WILD GOOSE CHASE

WILD GOOSE CHASE

Exploring the spirituality of everyday life

Annie Heppenstall

WILD GOOSE PUBLICATIONS
www.ionabooks.com

Copyright © 2006 Annie Heppenstall

First published 2006 by
Wild Goose Publications,
4th Floor, Savoy House, 140 Sauchiehall St, Glasgow G2 3DH, UK.
Wild Goose Publications is the publishing division of the Iona Community.
Scottish Charity No. SCO03794. Limited Company Reg. No. SCO96243.
www.ionabooks.com

ISBN 1-901557-94-4
13-digit ISBN: 978-1-901557-94-7

The publishers gratefully acknowledge the support of the Drummond Trust,
3 Pitt Terrace, Stirling FK8 2EY, in producing this book.

Cover design © Wild Goose Publications
Cover photograph © T. Vandersar /SuperStock
Internal illustrations © Annie Heppenstall

Annie Heppenstall has asserted her right under the Copyright, Designs and Patents Act,
1988 to be identified as the author of this work.

Overseas distribution:
Australia: Willow Connection Pty Ltd, Unit 4A, 3-9 Kenneth Road,
Manly Vale, NSW 2093
New Zealand: Pleroma, Higginson Street, Otane 4170, Central Hawkes Bay
Canada: Novalis/Bayard Publishing & Distribution, 10 Lower Spadina Ave.,
Suite 400, Toronto, Ontario M5V 2Z2

Printed by Bell & Bain, Thornliebank, Glasgow, Scotland

ACKNOWLEDGEMENTS

My main thanks go to everyone at All Hallows Church, Leeds. I discovered All Hallows in the process of writing *Wild Goose Chase*, and have found the community to be a ceaseless source of challenge and hope, and very much the space I needed. I am particularly indebted to Ray Gaston, currently priest to All Hallows, for giving so much encouragement, inspiration and support, and specifically for his innovative ideas about Christian forms of prayer in relation to Muslim prayer practice, which connected with and went beyond the 'Daniel Prayer' in chapter 6. I am also indebted to two different groups within the church. The first was instigated by Steve Thackray and James Jefferies, to try out and develop some liturgies I had put together. The outcome of one of these meetings, the Leaderless Eucharist, is included in chapter 8. So thanks especially to James and Steve, Phil, Moira, Isobel, Andrew, Ray and anyone else who came along. The second group included all who were part of the initiative to go prayer-walking around the parish, but in particular David, Isobel, Ray and Luke, who did the city prayer-walk with me, included (in a revised form) in chapter 7. I would also like to thank everyone who took part in the Christianity and Anarchism Conference hosted at All Hallows in 2006, especially Keith Hebden, for such a warm and encouraging response to the Leaderless Eucharist, which is now dedicated to Jesus radicals everywhere!

I am also indebted to Angela Hughes, for the wonderfully enriching conversations we had over coffee and during walks by the lakeside; to Jared, who although we later parted company gave the much appreciated material support I needed to be able to write the book; and to Luke our son, for sharing the computer with me very understandingly! I must also mention Sandra Kramer, Publishing Manager at Wild Goose Publications, who has been so patient and sensitive with me in getting this book ready for publication.

Contents

God in the ordinary, in marginalised people and work situations around us.
Raven as a symbol of Holy Spirit.

God in the home; Jesus in people's homes; symbolism and opportunity for reflection within the home.

God in meeting our needs, and our service of God through meeting the needs of others. The cockerel as a reflection on Peter's denial, his lowest point and moment of deepest need.

Communication with God – the eagle carries the prayers of the faithful.
Intercessory and Celtic-style prayers relating to situations in everyday life.

Being with God through cycles and passing of time; days and months.
Reflection on dying and rising.

Reflections on our physical bodies, and seeking opportunity to focus on the presence of God in the present moment.

The spiritual journey of our lives; seeking and finding a love relationship with God through contemplation.

Exploring communion; coming together for the 'lakeshore experience',
lakes being a point of contact between heaven and earth; a concluding act of worship – the Leaderless Eucharist.

How precious is your steadfast love, O God!
All people may take refuge in the shadow of your wings.

Psalm 36:7 (NRSV)

INTRODUCTION

Ask and it will be given you; search and you will find; knock and the door will be opened for you. For everyone who asks receives, and everyone who searches finds, and for everyone who knocks, the door will be opened.

Matthew 7:7-8

Wild Goose Chase draws on stories from the Bible and other sources to explore the journey each of us makes as we seek to live ordinary life in a spiritual way. Since prehistory, human beings have loved to share good stories, music and dancing, often around a fire as the night closes in. It is a time to dream, to laugh, to strengthen relationships. Story is an ancient and much-loved bearer of truth and, through the world of imagination and intuition, provides a refreshingly 'different' way of looking at life and religious experience. Our religious gatherings today are in their own way, I think, a tidied-up version of this innate sacredness of shared living and loving – at their best they are *alive*, reverberating with timeless depth of feeling and spiritual energy. And what greater story is there than that of the soul's journey to discover the God of Love?

I have called this book *Wild Goose Chase* for two main reasons. The first is the huge significance of birds in the mythology of cultures worldwide. Birds appear as spiritual beings or creatures sent angel-like by God to communicate divine messages, or to give healing, help and guidance. In the Bible, the dove is probably the most obvious example: she bears an olive branch as a sign that the flood waters are receding, and at the baptism of Jesus she descends as a symbol of the Holy Spirit. In Christian thinking the wild goose itself has come to be used by many, especially in the British Isles, as a rather rugged image of the Holy Spirit, a compelling, dynamic force that might believably drive a person into the wilderness to wrestle with temptation. The Shekinah (presence of God) is often represented as a mother bird, nestling her chicks. There are sparrows and swallows, both of whom build their homes in God's temple; there are ravens who bring food to a starving prophet; and eagles, admired for their power and clear sight, their flight a symbol of the prayers of the faithful soaring to heaven. There is the cockerel that reminded Peter of his failure, and the traditional use of the phoenix as a symbol of Christ's death and resurrection. Then we have the hawk-god Horus of the ancient Egyptians, the Native American Thunderbird, the creative raven, the Japanese peace crane, the Caribbean firebird who brings the sun each dawn, the healing birds of the Celtic myths who served the goddess Rhiannon, and the dove of Aphrodite, Greek goddess of love. The Romans too developed a whole divinatory practice based on the observation of sea birds by sailors, which progressed to the art of augury. Many shamanic cultures see birds as spirit guides: just as water birds can dive down into the depths of the water, so a shaman will, through ritual, seek to penetrate a person's inner being to reach the source of their sickness. It is healing through myth and symbol, through diving into the subconscious and addressing the heart of the problem: the dis-ease of the soul rather than the mechanics of the body.

The birds then, blessed with mobility through air, over land and sometimes deep into water too, have been seen as symbolic messengers between the world of spirit and human consciousness, and we can still use them today in our contemplation. With this theme, *Wild Goose Chase* goes deep into various areas of life – our self-perception, our bodies, our relationships, our experience of worship, our place in the days and seasons of the year, the daily activities we are engaged in – and offers reflections on these in the context of our search for the God of Love.

The other reason for the title *Wild Goose Chase* is the meaning of the phrase itself. *The Concise Oxford Dictionary* defines a wild goose chase as a 'foolish and unproductive quest': it is as difficult to achieve the objective as it is to catch a wild goose. Paul, in his first letter to the Corinthians, described the way of the cross as 'foolishness to those who are perishing'. Since Christianity began, it has made little sense to a lot of people; even most of Jesus's disciples seem often to have failed to understand him. In the gospels we catch glimpses of understanding from unexpected individuals: a wise Jewish scribe who is near to the Kingdom because of his insight into the importance of love; a woman's (Martha's) statement that Jesus is Messiah; a Roman centurion's complete confidence in the authority of Jesus; a village woman anointing Jesus's head with oil, in a prophetic gesture of king-making. But, on the whole, the way of love and self-giving seems to make no sense. There is a strong feeling that those who believe such promises as the one quoted at the head of the chapter are deluding themselves, accepting an opiate from a controlling institution, allowing themselves to tolerate misery in this life in the hope of something better in the next. It does seem like foolishness to turn away from pursuit of wealth, prestige and power – all the 'goodness' that material existence can offer. For what meaning can there be to life other than the obvious – to prosper and enjoy ourselves while we have the chance? How can there be any point to anything, except to self-interest? Yet, some people do seek a path other than the normal one of selfish, material gain, and in seeking they find what is worthwhile. These people stand out because they have something profound to give others. *Wild Goose Chase* is an exploration of the promise that if we seek we will find, in the process of our daily lives.

Chapter 1

THE RAVEN

~ and he breathed on them

About this chapter

This is a book about finding spirituality in the ordinary things of everyday life, and this chapter begins with some of the people whom we meet in the Bible and as we go about our lives, including the ones we might sometimes prefer to avoid: the marginalised, those labelled as unclean, unacceptable to polite society, the failures, the drop-outs, the diseased, the losers ...

In the culture of Jesus's day, the ordinary people who spent their lives toiling away in the fields, and at all the vital occupations which provided the food and resources for the population at large, were pejoratively referred to as *am ha-arez: peasants*. The whole of the population of Galilee tended to be lumped together under this derogatory title, their understanding of cultic law thought to be particularly lax. The *am ha-arez* tended to be uneducated and therefore ignorant of the complexities of the law in all its detail; their religion would be an abbreviated form which revolved around the celebration of agricultural festivals, an occasional pilgrimage to the temple, varying knowledge of Bible stories and prayers, and perhaps observance at some level of the Friday night family meal and the command to rest on the sabbath. People who lived off the labour of the *am ha-arez* despised them for the imperfection of their worship, and avoided social contact with them.

It is to these people that Jesus belonged: he was a Galilean, he was *am ha-arez*, and he spent most of his ministry travelling around the villages where they lived, spreading the good news that they were acceptable to God and welcome in God's kingdom. Jesus was a man of the ordinary people – the workers, the peasants, the marginalised, the despised – and still is. His message was that all are called to be God's holy people, not just the ones who because of their station in life can dedicate themselves to perfect devotion. Christianity began as a hands-on approach for working people to living an ordinary life in a spiritual way.

We still have our marginalised and despised members of society. Sometimes we enter into that marginalisation ourselves and feel what it is like to be powerless, vulnerable and exploited. We still have structures which raise some people up as godly, and put others down as ignorant, ungodly or less worthy. Some of these people are conveniently outside our immediate communities: sweatshop workers, gem miners ... people we can pretend not to see as we go about our consumerism. But they are as valuable to God as we are. Jesus is for them as much as he is for us.

The story

The raven is the first bird to appear in the Bible. Her story goes like this. It had been raining hard for longer than anyone could remember and the ark, which must have seemed huge when it was being built, now felt cramped, noisy and squalid; the people and the creatures within needed to get out into the fresh air again or soon life would no longer be worth living. But God remembered the boat bobbing helplessly on the surface of the floodwaters, and sent a wind – the same wind that swept over the waters before the beginning of time: Ruah, the sacred breath of God. This powerful wind moved the rain clouds on and let the waters draw back to reveal land once more. Eventually the ark came to rest on the top of the tallest of mountains, and after forty days Noah decided it was time to open up the hatch in the roof. Going to the coops and cages he had made to house the animals, something made him open up the ravens' cage, and out flew the female, straight through the hatch, without a backward glance. Why did he choose the raven? Who knows? I wouldn't be surprised if hers was the loud voice that had been annoying him the most and he wanted to be rid of her.

So out of the hatch the raven flew, and once she was set loose she never came back but flew endlessly over the huge expanse, wild and hungry but preferring her wildness and her hunger to captivity. And, so the story says, the raven flew back and forth over the deep until all the waters had dried up. Scholars of the Talmud will tell you that that was not until the day when a terrible drought hit the land of Israel, because of the misdeeds of a powerful king called Ahab. Elijah was a prophet at that time, sent by God to speak truth to Ahab and make him change his ways for the sake of the people. Elijah took refuge in the wilderness during the drought, and it was the raven that God sent to bring him food.

Comment

In Genesis 1:1–2, it is Ruah, the breath of God, which sweeps over the face of the endless waters before God creates even light. In the story of the flood, the breath or the wind comes back to stop the rain, and then it is the raven who flies to and fro over the waters: breath of God, Ruah, raven, somehow connected. This is a challenging connection to make, because the raven, according to the priestly law code, is an unclean creature as it eats carrion (and according to the Talmud it was the male raven who was thrown out of the ark for breaking a taboo on sexual relations while afloat!).

Yet everything that God makes in creation is good. At the beginning of time there is neither clean nor unclean. Even eating carrion is acceptable – it is part of the regenerative cycle which God established for the preservation of life. What came later to be despised is here declared to be of God, and with a purpose. The black raven, freedom-seeker, is beautiful and somehow becomes identified with the Sacred Breath which carries the voice of God.

And not unlike those who bear the truth, the raven becomes the object of marginalisation, an outcast, unclean. And not unlike those who bear the truth, she, as she reappears in a later Bible story, in going to feed Elijah in the desert, becomes the one who sees the need of another creature and meets that need. The one who already lives on the edge, the one who speaks with a voice that nobody wants to hear, perhaps has a greater affinity with those who find themselves in trouble than does the one who has always lived in unchallenged comfort.

The raven then, in the Bible, is an enigmatic character. Those who seek meaning have connected the dove, as a pure and gentle symbol, to the breath of God, Holy Spirit; but it is the raven that echoes the potent movement of that breath. She is a deep and subversive symbol of the voice of God which we hear through the marginalised, the unloved and the ostracised. It is the voice we most need to hear, and most often resist: with the voice of the raven speaks Christ.

Soul friend

I see Mary, mother of Jesus, as the lady of the raven. Mary, we are told, was made aware by the prophecy of Simeon in the temple that she would outlive her son. In many cultures, as typified in the Norse legends for example, the raven is an omen of death; it was naturally attracted by the gore of battlegrounds, so there was an element of horror in its presence. Mary's knowledge overshadowed the whole of Jesus's life. Did she ever tell him about it, or did she keep it to herself?

In the Magnificat we meet Mary as a strong-minded and politically intelligent woman, giving voice to her awareness of the hunger of her people – God's people – for justice, equality and mercy. She knew and understood, and she passed that political awareness on to her son. In the Apocryphal books of the Maccabees we read of another mother who watched not one son die but five, at the hands of the occupying force. Tortured as she was by seeing their suffering, she exhorted them to endure rather than give up their faith. Mary is often portrayed as a meek, passive woman, pitifully weeping, a victim of circumstances beyond her control. But there must have been an element of the immense courage and faith of that Maccabean mother in Mary. To utter such a strong political statement at the beginning of Jesus's life cries out for an equally impassioned response to his death. In Mary's heart there was surely a deeper understanding that what her son was doing was noble and brave and right, and so her grief was tinged with a real sense of pride in the stand he had taken. She was there for him at the foot of the cross; she must have been a woman of some mettle to watch that death. Her presence there was, perhaps, her last statement of support for her son, she who had fed him her own wisdom and insight, and watched him as he followed his convictions to their natural conclusion. To the end she gave him what he needed: her approval of his decision to embrace death for the sake of the message of a kingdom of peace. Mary is the bearer of insurmountable grief, the one who nourished the heart and mind of Christ, and voice of the lowly – the ordinary person – crying out the needs of the world for justice and peace. It is a voice that is often ignored.

Contemplation on God's people through poetry

With the lives of the ordinary and the marginalised at heart, three passages from the Old Testament spring to mind. The first is a warning which God gives through Samuel, the last of the great judges of Israel; the second is about the warning coming true; and the third, in two parts, describes Elijah, a prophet who is prepared to speak God's truth for the sake of the oppressed. We can draw out each person's story in a way that still speaks to us today. The examples I have offered below use a Japanese form of poetry called haiku, which follows a beautifully simple structure of counted syllables for each line, always five, then seven, then five. Being so concise, these lines are written to express the essence of a matter, in particular to shed fresh light on something quite ordinary. When meditating on a theme, haiku is an ideal way to express an insight without the clutter of words. Have a go!

So Samuel reported all the words of the Lord to the people who were asking him for a king. He said, 'These will be the ways of the king who will reign over you: he will take your sons and appoint them to his chariots and to be his horsemen, and to run before his chariots; and he will appoint for himself commanders of thousands and commanders of fifties, and some to plough his ground and to reap his harvest, and to make his implements of war and the equipment of his chariots. He will take your daughters to be perfumers and cooks and bakers. He will take the best of your fields and vineyards and olive orchards and give them to his courtiers. He will take one-tenth of your grain and of your vineyards and give it to his officers and his courtiers. He will take your male and female slaves, and the best of your cattle and donkeys, and put them to his work. He will take one-tenth of your flocks, and you shall be his slaves.'

1 Samuel 8:10–17

Samuel, the last of the Judges of Israel, or any elderly person …
Old I am and wise:
God is your king, and no man.
But you do not hear.

The mother of a conscripted soldier
Power games of kings
rob us, death's shadow threatens,
we grieve wasted life.

A subsistence farmer with a family to feed
My children hunger
to be fed; what food I grow
is not ours to eat.

A girl slave, corn-grinder for the king
Dull work, muscles ache,
my life sold for a pittance,
I am so weary

The second group of characters comes from an account describing Solomon's building programme.

King Solomon conscripted forced labour out of all Israel; the levy numbered thirty thousand men. He sent them to the Lebanon, ten thousand a month in shifts; they would be a month in the Lebanon and two months at home; Adoniram was in charge of the forced labour. Solomon also had seventy thousand labourers and eighty thousand stonecutters in the hill country, besides Solomon's three thousand three hundred supervisors who were over the work, having charge of the people who did the work. At the king's command, they quarried out great, costly stones in order to lay the foundation of the house with dressed stones.

1 Kings 5:13–17

A quarry worker
No God of justice
will live in a house built by
my exploitation.

A tree-cutter in Lebanon
Ancient, noble trees
felled by my axe, all gone now,
bare hills seem bereft.

Adoniram, chief officer in charge of forced labour
I'm just obeying
orders to subjugate my
brothers; don't blame me.

Wife of a worker, away for one month in three
I do his work too,
how else can the children eat?
God, free your people.

The third group draws on stories concerning Elijah, King Ahab and Queen Jezebel. The passages are too long to include the entire text, so I have provided excerpts. For the full account read 1 Kings 16:29–21:29.

Ahab did more to provoke the anger of the Lord, the God of Israel, than had all the kings of Israel who were before him. In his days Hiel of Bethel built Jericho; he laid its foundation at the cost of Abiram his firstborn, and set up its gates at the cost of his youngest son Segub, according to the word of the Lord, which he spoke by Joshua son of Nun. Now Elijah the Tishbite, of Tishbe in Gilead, said to Ahab, 'As the Lord the God of Israel lives, before whom I stand, there shall be neither dew nor rain these years, except by my word.' The word of the Lord came to him, saying, 'Go from here and turn eastwards, and hide yourself by the Wadi Cherith, which is east of the Jordan. You shall drink from the wadi, and I have commanded the ravens to feed you there.'
1 Kings 16:33–17

Then they sent to Jezebel, saying, 'Naboth has been stoned; he is dead.' As soon as Jezebel heard that Naboth had been stoned and was dead, Jezebel said to Ahab, 'Go, take possession of the vineyard of Naboth the Jezreelite, which he refused to give you for money; for Naboth is not alive, but dead.' As soon as Ahab heard that Naboth was dead, Ahab set out to go down to the vineyard of Naboth the Jezreelite, to take possession of it.
1 Kings 21:14–16

Elijah, prophet of God
Afraid or not, I
will not witness injustice
then ignore God's voice.

Ahab
I hate that prophet.
I am king, all power is mine,
I am my own god.

Jezebel
Luxury, power,
what other purpose is there
but to serve myself?

Naboth's widow
Cruel empire grows as
innocent blood, shed for greed
cries out from the land.

Extending the contemplation

Having spent time with the biblical characters, we can move on to the people around us, to feel for them, to try to gain a picture of their life situation, to see them with compassion and empathy. How might their stories be expressed through the same form of haiku poetry? How might you express your own story as you see it today? How might somebody else see your story?

Writing, I reach out,
exploring the word of God;
who will share my thoughts?

Celebrating the ordinary

The accounts above draw us into the lives of real people – unnamed and ordinary, perhaps, but timeless. Somehow, as old as these stories are, still we know them and can identify with them. The Bible is a living book and the people within it speak to us. There has been a suggestion, through the centuries, that seeking God is for those who have the time, those who commit themselves to holy orders and can hand over the tasks of everyday life to others, while they themselves offer up their prayers and meditations to God on behalf of those who do not have time. It creates a two-tier approach to spirituality: the faith of the laity, which is often reduced to devotion and dependence on a priesthood, and the faith of the truly religious, the ones who are learned in scripture, with space to exercise the disciplines of the more 'perfect' way.

But we all have free access to God. This is a truth that people in the past have been prepared to go to gaol to proclaim. Whatever priesthood is about, it is not about having a special hotline to God, nor is it about practising a higher form of devotion. Perhaps it is harder for an ordinary person living an everyday life to be true to faith than it is for one from whom this is expected because of an ordained role, but it does not mean that we cannot live by our faith every minute of the day if we choose to. Asceticism and withdrawal from the world is one way, but not the only way. Jesus came to the villagers, the ordinary people, and he didn't call them to celibacy, self-mortification or rigorous prayer routines. He shed new light on the lives they were already living, that they might continue, enriched by a renewed sense of courageous, self-giving love. He talked about attitude as much as practice – the calling of all God's people, not just the ones who set themselves up as pure and righteous.

Jesus and the prophets all pointed to everyday occupations to offer insight into the nature of God; in their teachings we find potters, bakers, gardeners, builders, sweepers and shepherds, to name but a few: hands-on, often dirty, tedious, thankless tasks, but ones in which insight into God can still be found.

Ordinary working life need not be a compulsory detour into secularism just because we have to do that embarrassingly unspiritual thing called *earning money*; it can be a valuable act of service, a sacrifice of time, a means to live out the love of God in everyday life and to reach out to others, wherever and with whomever we are. Here then are some reflections on the work of God's people in scripture. We may be able to identify with some of them, whether we are employed in particular occupations, find ourselves doing them anyway, or have indirect experience. While we are often defined by our job, we in fact do many of the things in this list in our own ways, and in each of them there is an opportunity for contemplation.

The Administrator

Joseph was thirty years old when he entered the service of Pharaoh king of Egypt. And Joseph went out from the presence of Pharaoh, and went through all the land of Egypt. During the seven plenteous years the earth produced abundantly. He gathered up all the food of the seven years when there was plenty in the land of Egypt, and stored up food in the cities; he stored up in every city the food from the fields around it. So Joseph stored up grain in such abundance – like the sand of the sea – that he stopped measuring it; it was beyond measure. The seven years of plenty that prevailed in the land of Egypt came to an end; and the seven years of famine began to come, just as Joseph had said. There was famine in every country, but throughout the land of Egypt there was bread. When all the land of Egypt was famished, the people cried to Pharaoh for bread. Pharaoh said to all the Egyptians, 'Go to Joseph; what he says to you, do.' And since the famine had spread over all the land, Joseph opened all the storehouses, and sold to the Egyptians, for the famine was severe in the land of Egypt. Moreover, all the world came to Joseph in Egypt to buy grain, because the famine became severe throughout the world.

Genesis 41:46–49, 53–57

Comment

The story of Joseph is one of a rather tactless boy, his father's favourite, who is attacked by his jealous brothers and sold as a slave. After ending up in prison in Egypt for a crime he did not commit, he finds that he can give wise counsel to fellow prisoners, and finally comes to the attention of the Pharaoh, who respects his wisdom and sets him up as chief administrator over national provisions in anticipation of a famine. At many points throughout Joseph's life, he seems to have been abandoned and is in despair, but in the end he is used by God to save the lives of thousands of people through the careful organisation of resources. His ability becomes an opportunity to serve.

What do you find yourself responsible for? For whose benefit is the intended outcome?

The Builder

Unless the Lord builds the house,
Those who build it labour in vain.
Psalm 127:1 NRSV

Comment

The implication is that labour is pointless, futile, unless it is blessed by God. We might think of the rich man in Luke 12:16 who built great storehouses to keep his wealth, only to be called 'fool' by God; and of the prophetic words of Jesus concerning the destruction of the temple (Mark 14:59) and the accusation brought against him that he had claimed he would build another in three days; surely an assertion of divinity. Jesus's own parable about building perhaps also reflects this sentiment: a house built on shifting sand will collapse in hard times; but the one who comes to Jesus, hears his words and acts on them 'is like a man building a house, who dug deeply and laid the foundation on a rock' (Luke 6:48).

What do you build up? On what foundations do you build?

The Baker

And again he said, 'To what should I compare the kingdom of God? It is like yeast that a
woman took and mixed in with three measures of flour until all of it was leavened.'
Luke 13:20–21 NRSV (also Matthew)

Jesus's use of yeast as a simile of the kingdom of God is interesting because its normal connotation for his contemporaries would have been very different. Here, Jesus refers to the quality of growth, and the way in which yeast in the form of already leavened dough was hidden in new dough so that it could be kneaded into the whole, thus enabling the bread to rise. We infer this meaning in part by reading it in the context of the story that immediately precedes it in Luke: the parable of the mustard seed, which is small but when planted becomes a large bush. The more usual understanding of yeast, or leaven, in the Bible is as something corrupt in its essence because of the process of fermentation – and thus breaking-down or decay – that has to take place before yeast can become active. So, the fleeing Hebrew slaves ate unleavened bread partly because of their haste, but also as a symbol of purity. Likewise, only unleavened bread was normally acceptable as an offering on the altar. This sense of the word sheds light on the warning in Matthew

16:6, to beware the yeast of the Pharisees and Sadducees: they were corrupt.

Ancient minds were quick to associate decay with pollution and defilement, partly for the good of their own health. We now accept, however, that this process is essential to the continuation of life on earth. Thus, in yeast we find a symbol for the regenerative cycle itself, the physical relationship between growth, death, decay and new life. But in the parable of the yeast in the bread, we must remember that Jesus is talking not about a physical, finite thing, but about a spiritual phenomenon. For the other term used of the kingdom of heaven is 'eternal life': life that is not limited by physical laws, because it is not of the physical world but of the realm of spirit.

What meaning does the cycle of growth, death, decay and new life have for you?

The Cleaner

When the unclean spirit has gone out of a person, it wanders through waterless regions looking for a resting place, but it finds none. Then it says, 'I will return to my house from which I came.' When it comes, it finds it empty, swept, and put in order. Then it goes and brings along seven other spirits more evil than itself, and they enter and live there; and the last state of that person is worse than the first. So will it be also with this evil generation.

Matt 12:43–45

Comment

A house may be cleaned and put in order after the departure of an unwelcome demon-guest, but it's no good leaving the house empty. It must be filled with a spirit that will deter the demon from returning. It's not good to live in a negative, destructive environment, but having realised and dealt with that, we can't just remain neutral. We have to take action, to be on guard against unwanted influences and fill our house, our mind, our heart, with love.

What state is your mind-house in?

The Gardener

I am the true vine, and my Father is the vine-grower. He removes every branch in me that bears no fruit. Every branch that bears fruit he prunes to make it bear more fruit.
John 15:1–6

For the land that you are about to enter to occupy is not like the land of Egypt, from which you have come, where you sow your seed and irrigate by foot like a vegetable garden. But the land that you are crossing over to occupy is a land of hills and valleys, watered by rain from the sky, a land that the Lord your God looks after. The eyes of the Lord your God are always on it, from the beginning of the year to the end of the year.
Deut 11:10–12

Comment

The Hebrew ex-slaves, accustomed to the artificial irrigation system of rainless Egypt, feel that God himself is tending the rain-watered hills of Canaan. To them, God is bound up with the weather, with the natural cycles and seasons, the success of the crops and the health of the people. To God is the glory for all, not the idols of the Canaanite people, who worship what they do not understand with empty rituals and meaningless effigies, caught up in gruesome, violent and meaningless practices. God holds all people in care. Jesus took this idea of God as the great power behind the natural world and brought out the spiritual dimension: as a gardener shapes a fruit tree to be productive, so God shapes us.

Have you ever had the sensation of being spiritually pruned?

The Midwife

The king of Egypt said to the Hebrew midwives, one of whom was named Shiphrah and the other Puah, 'When you act as midwives to the Hebrew women, and see them on the birthstool, if it is a boy, kill him; but if it is a girl, she shall live.' But the midwives feared God; they did not do as the king of Egypt commanded them, but they let the boys live. So the king of Egypt summoned the midwives and said to them, 'Why have you done this, and allowed the boys to live?' The midwives said to Pharaoh, 'Because the Hebrew women are not like the Egyptian women; for they are vigorous and give birth before the midwife comes to them.' So God dealt well with the midwives; and the people multiplied and became very strong. And because the midwives feared God, he gave them families.

Exodus 1:15–21

Comment

The midwives are a resistance movement among the Hebrews. They know what is good and right and they stick to it, in defiance of the authorities. They do not succumb to the famous excuse for atrocities: *'I was only obeying orders.'* So the Egyptians have to think again about how to control the population.

When do you bring forth goodness in the face of opposition?

The Carpenter

'Is not this the carpenter, the son of Mary and brother of James and Joses and Judas and Simon, and are not his sisters here with us?' And they took offence at him.

Mark 6:33

Comment

Jesus was a carpenter, with skills and understanding which he had learned from his own father. Much has been written, often of a romantic nature, about Jesus's strong carpenter's hands and so on. We don't know if he was any good at it though. After all, he did give it up to take up a preaching ministry! But he was part of the tradition of artisans, to which Paul also belonged with his tent-making skills. Paul himself recommended that people have a handcraft to fall back on in order to support themselves and not depend on charity as they went about their work for Christ. These days, he might advise us to be computer literate. Then, the ability to make something by hand was valued. It meant you could occupy a niche in society, supplying a need. Jesus was rejected by his home town because it seemed he was setting out to be something other than what he was: he was the village carpenter so why was he setting himself up as a religious teacher? That was somebody else's job. By breaking the mould he lost respect. He gave up his 'niche', his accepted role in the community, and became somebody on the edge. The people of the community considered him a fool, because he had given up security and livelihood to pursue a vocation that was not his, and it was not his because it was not the vocation he had learned from his father. To them, he had no authority.

Do you feel that a niche has been moulded for you? Does it suit you? Does it ever feel as though other people's expectations of you need to be challenged, so that you can move on?

The Teacher

You call me Teacher and Lord – and you are right, for that is what I am. So if I, your Lord and Teacher, have washed your feet, you also ought to wash one another's feet.
John 13:13–14

Not many of you should become teachers, my brothers and sisters, for you know that we who teach will be judged with greater strictness.
James 3:1

Comment

Jesus was the teacher par excellence. When we set out to share our faith as far as we understand it, he cautions us against pretending we know and understand more than we do. Once we put ourselves in the position of having authority, then we open ourselves to criticism. What if we are wrong? What if the other person has a greater insight? Yet it is also our duty to share with one another, to support each other in our faith, to move one another on and allow ourselves to be moved on. The crux of the matter is whom to trust. Are we trustworthy? Do we keep silence out of modesty when really what we have to say might be helpful to somebody? Do we say too much and reveal our ignorance?

Whom do you trust to guide you?

Closing prayer

Great Spirit of All,
In my daily life, as many people come and go,
remind me that in each of them breathes your holiness.
Touch my encounters with the wide wings of your power,
that as each person's story unfolds before me,
so may grow my love.
Inspire me to seek out those stories
from the ones who need to be heard.
Give me patience to listen
and in listening, to hear your voice
deep at the heart of the energy of life.
Living Breath and Voice of Truth,
cry out in me for the sake of the voiceless;
and draw me to the edge,
to the wilderness places
where prophets wait to be fed.
Amen

Chapter 2

THE DOVE

~ We will come to them and make our home with them

About this chapter

This chapter looks again at the Holy Spirit, in the context of the home. Home is naturally a very important place in all cultures, and in many it has become the preserve of women. So there is a strong feminine element to this chapter, which is centred around the symbol of the dove. She makes her home where she is made welcome, and where she is free to come and go. The Holy Spirit is gentle but she is also wild, not something we can trap and keep for ourselves. Our place of belonging is nestled under the wings of the mother bird, Holy Spirit, Shekinah, God our Mother: Psalm 17:8, *Guard me as the apple of your eye, hide me in the shadow of your wings …* The Shekinah is described in various ways but is generally understood as the female, dynamic Spirit of God which is present in creation; it is a concept explored in mystical branches of Judaism, and can also be identified with Ruah, breath of God, or Holy Spirit.

This Shekinah, or presence of God, loves human beings and has always dwelt among them. The Hebrews of the exodus made a tabernacle to house the ark, where her presence hovered as a cloud by day and fire by night. She settles among the people, as a breath of God. Wisdom is another of her names. She is with Jesus and in Jesus from his baptism, and she is with us and in us, if we follow Jesus's teaching to love one another, for Jesus gave us the Spirit to be with us. In John 20:22 we read that he breathed the Spirit upon his disciples; Jesus gave the Breath of God literally – Ruah was within him.

So in this chapter I work with the concept of 'home', especially our own homes and special places as dwellings which reflect our sense of the presence of God, and our sacred spaces, wherever we are. I explore this through people in Bible stories with whom we might identify, who welcomed Jesus into their homes; through the insights of other cultures, which can speak to our own sense of spirituality; and through contemplating the spaces and places in our own homes.

The story

It had been raining a long, long time when God remembered Noah and his menagerie. When the rain stopped, the first bird Noah released, hoping it would show him whether the land was dry or not, was the raven, but the raven just flew off and never came back. So then Noah took a dove. Perhaps he thought the dove was more likely to do what he wanted than the wild raven; the dove was quite settled in the ark, in her little pigeon-hole snuggled up with her mate and all the grain she wanted to eat; she would come back. He found the dove gentle and willing, and let her loose through the hatchway of the ark quite confidently. And off she flew. Now, finding no land, the dove did come back, and descending from the skies she alighted on the hand which Noah held out for her, and let herself be brought back inside. Seven days passed and Noah sent her out once more. This time she came back with an olive leaf in her beak, not for Noah, but to make a nest in the ark that was her home. But Noah didn't think about her desire for nest-building, and having got the information he wanted, he shut the hatch and fastened the door of the dove cage, and never thought any more about her. But, with her natural instincts awoken, the dove pined to be let out again, and when seven days later Noah came back to use her again, this time – like the raven – she flew off and never came back. She would make a nest in freedom; no more living on Noah's terms.

Comment

The dove is made use of because she is quite tame; she is let out, gets a taste of freedom, remembers what her life is for and sets about finding what she needs to get on with it. Trusting, she comes back, and then is trapped, not out of malevolence but out of human thoughtlessness or lack of imagination. Only one thing matters to Noah, and that is to know when he can leave the ark. But the price for denying the dove the little freedom she wants from him – just to come and go as she pleases with her leaves and twigs – is that she leaves him completely.

The dove has become a symbol of the Holy Spirit through the description of Jesus's baptism, where the Holy Spirit descended and alighted on him *like a dove*. This dove-like spirit which alights on Jesus is an echo of the dove coming back to the ark, full of trust and willingness. The dove which left Noah has come back to Jesus. With Noah, there was constraint: she was being used and she wasn't free to make her home in peace. With Jesus there is freedom: here the Spirit will make her home. Jesus will hold her lightly, never trap her, never use her for his own ends; he will respect her and let her be a source of joy to him. And in a way, Jesus is like the dove too, and Jesus is the dove. Jesus will try to make his home with us, and it is up to us how we respond. Do we shut the door on him? Or, once we think we have him, lock him in, and hold on to him so tightly there is no breath left? Or do we let him move freely and creatively within us?

Soul friends

Among the many who show hospitality to Jesus, there are two sisters who welcome Jesus into their house, Mary and Martha. He comes and goes, it seems, and they hold his love lightly and lovingly between them. I equate these sisters with the dove; between them they offer a kind of balance of opposites. In the account of Lazarus's death and raising, Martha goes out to confront Jesus, but Mary stays at home. In the story of Jesus's visit, Mary is indoors and sits close to listen to him talking while Martha is in and out, busy with her own agenda. Mary seems gentle, but not I think in a subservient way. She claims her place to hear the word of the teacher, when the duty expected of her by society is to serve; she is quietly self-confident and not a little subversive. And she it is, it seems, who took expensive perfume, and 'wasted' it, in the opinion of Jesus's disciples, in a gesture of love, an act of foot-washing which Jesus was then to repeat for his own disciples. The writer of John's gospel says she poured it out over Jesus's feet, while in Mark, although the woman is not named, the story is very much the same except that she pours the oil over Jesus's head. She performs the ancient prophetic role of the king-maker. Whatever else anybody might say about Jesus from then on, nothing could change the fact that he has been anointed, by a woman, in her home. Mary of Bethany anoints Jesus the king, and Martha proclaims him to be king, Messiah! These then are friends of all who break the mould, knowing that relationship to Christ and responsiveness to his presence must be put before convention and the expectations of others. They are with us in our homes.

Who lets Jesus into their homes?

The gospel stories have many accounts of people encountering Jesus in their own homes. This was where Jesus came to meet people, and where much of his healing and teaching took place. In particular it was easier for him to encounter women in the home, as this was their domain. In Mark's gospel homes are the location for a lot of activity; often Jesus is described as being 'at home' in Capernaum, which is quite likely to mean 'at Peter's home'. Matthew, who often uses Mark's material, has Jesus out and about much more and often either does not tell us where an event takes place or has it in public or on the road. Luke, who also uses Mark's material, has a number of unique accounts of Jesus visiting people; several of these set the stage for debates with Pharisees. John's approach is rather more like Matthew's: there is only one specific account of a house-visit, but that is a very significant one, where he is anointed by a woman.

Here, then, to take us into the theme of Christ in the home, is a series of reflections in the form of stories as they might be told by characters in the gospels – an approach inspired by but not particularly emulating what is known as Ignatian contemplation, where a biblical character and their situation is imagined, as an aid to drawing closer to the heart of scripture. We each see people in a different way of course, so the following are invitations to a creative meditation rather than expressions of 'the way it was'.

Levi brings Jesus home for a dodgy party

Mark 2:13–17

I am Levi, although some people call me Matthew. I used to have a desk in the tax office at the side of the market place, and here I would sit every day, the sounds of the sellers, the musicians, the beggars, the animals and the preachers in the background. Tax-collecting is not a popular job, but we all have to work, and it pays well; you just have to be a bit thick-skinned. One particular day, I was half-listening as I worked to the voice of a man who had attracted a big crowd; he was talking about the kingdom of God, a state of peace reached through looking out for one another instead of living in our own little self-interested worlds; the spiritual riches of life instead of material wealth. As I dealt with the people one by one, sullen and disgruntled at having to part with their hard-earned incomes, I was responding to him in my head, almost justifying myself really. But I have to say the job had been wearing me down a bit. It's hard when nobody likes you at all. The only friends I'd got were people in the same line as me, and they were a pretty hard-faced lot. Being well paid did mean it was easy to pick up women of course. Half-starved some of them were. They would sell themselves for the price of a meal – pitiful, but I wasn't complaining at the time. I told myself I was doing them a favour, magnanimous me. I pretended I was having the time of my life, but really my life was empty; there just wasn't a spiritual side to it.

Well, the preacher stopped for lunch I suppose in the end, and I got back to my queue of grumpy people. Some time later, at the tail end of the line, I noticed a little posse of shabby-looking friends who stood out because they seemed so good humoured. Most people who were waiting had nothing to laugh about at all. As they approached my desk the leader strode forward, full of confidence, and for a moment I wondered whether he was coming to cause trouble – some nationalist with his heavy guys, protesting about the empire again. We get a lot of that. So many people hate the occupation, and hate the Romans bleeding us dry, that anyone who accepts a job from the Romans is seen as betraying the cause. So I started to get a bit edgy. He looked straight at me, and I was surprised to find that he had no aggression about him, only self-assurance. 'Follow me,' he said. 'Come, follow me.' As he spoke I realised he was the man who had been preaching in the market earlier: Jesus. A sudden desire for freedom came over me and I just got up from my desk and went with him.

That night I offered to put him and his friends up at my place. I was a bit worried he'd say no. For a moment I felt ashamed of who my friends were. But they were no worse than me, and it seemed like in coming to me he was coming to all of us; why single me out for special attention? So I called up all the people I could find – work colleagues mainly, and some of the women I had been 'looking after', as I called it – and we had a great party. My friends made a disreputable bunch, I have to say, but they loved Jesus. He seemed the kind of person who could get on with anybody – good sense of humour. And they heard him out too, and some of them, you could see, were really listening. So I was glad I'd brought him home. That's nearly the end of the story, except that much later in the night these guys crashed the party, wanting to meet Jesus. They'd heard him preaching too, and they'd come for a discussion; ultra-religious types, they were. But when they saw Jesus sitting surrounded by prostitutes and tax-collectors, they had a real go at him. I suppose it didn't look very good. I thought he would get a bit defensive, be embarrassed at getting caught at a dodgy party, but he didn't. He told them we'd got a better idea of what it's all about than they had with their self-righteous hypocrisy, and if they were so sure they'd got it all wrapped up, why were they wasting their time looking for Jesus anyway? Beat that! I've followed him ever since!

Related stories

Luke 19:1–10 Jesus eats with Zacchaeus.

John 4:1–42 After Jesus's conversation with a Samaritan woman by a well, he stays with the Samaritans for two days.

Simon the Pharisee invites Jesus to dinner

Luke 7:36–50

I am Simon. I am a Pharisee – that means my family and I try to live an ordinary life in a holy way. I follow the laws God gave us, because they are there to be followed. This makes me feel that I know where I am, that I'm pleasing God, and it keeps my mind centred on the spiritual rather than the secular. There is a rule or a tradition for everything; serving God permeates every part of life.

A while ago I heard about Jesus, this maverick young teacher who seemed to have appeared from nowhere, certainly not from one of the rabbinic schools, nor from any of our leading families; there seemed to be no authority behind him to give weight to his teaching, except that he had some connection with the preacher John the Baptist. Now, John was very well respected as a man of God, but Jesus isn't like him. He doesn't practise asceticism – quite the opposite, from what I'd heard: it sounded as though he was a bit of a waster, wandering round abusing people's hospitality and giving our religion a bad name. People were saying he could heal the sick, and that didn't help; I have always been somewhat suspicious of charismatic healers, I have to say. There are so many charlatans around, pretending to work through God's power, but just taking advantage of people's credulity. When he appeared in the area, I thought I'd have him round. Who knows – perhaps I might put him right on a few points, let him see the value in quietly living by the book, calm him down a bit, show him what a good life he could have if he just settled to a trade and stopped drawing attention to himself. So I sent and invited him to dinner.

Well, dinner didn't get off to a very good start. First, he just stood there in the doorway with half a dozen of his shabby friends, obviously having made no attempt to dress for the occasion. They just kicked their sandals off at the door and walked in, heading straight inside as though they owned the place, yet none of them looked as though they had ever lived in anything better than a fisherman's hut. None of the formalities, the little courtesies guests usually exchange with hosts, no gift-giving. Ignorant, I call it. It just showed him up for the peasant he is, some northern villager with no idea of how to behave in polite society. So that set my back up straight away, and I decided to play him at his own game, and 'accidentally' forgot the foot-washing.

Well he sat down, he and his friends, looking around the room. My house is quite tastefully decorated, though I say so myself, and I was quite pleased that he would see from the ornaments and the expensive rugs what kind of man he was dealing with, how well blessed I have been. He didn't say anything though, and that irritated me, although he did seem to enjoy the food. He complimented my wife for that instead of me. That really annoyed me too; women know not to speak to strange men, so he put her in a really awkward position. She blushed and looked down, but she was smiling none the less. I spoke to her about that afterwards.

Well, anyway, I threw questions at him as challenges rather than to make conversation, resenting his ever coming into my house with his bad manners. But I didn't really feel that I was getting anywhere. I wasn't going to get him to change his attitude. There was an obstinacy about him, or a self-assurance, that I thought was completely unjustified: who did he think he was, talking as though he knew the mind of God?

As we ate, passers-by wandered in from the street to see if there was any food going, or if there was anything interesting to listen to. That's the norm here: we keep an open door when we entertain, and people can come in; it's one of our ways of giving alms to the poor. One woman sidled in and stood nervously, leaning against the wall. I admit I knew who she was well enough, and didn't particularly want her embarrassing me in my house, eyeing up the guests. She stood there staring at Jesus, and I called a servant to remove her. Just as the servant approached her she darted away, but instead of running out of the door she ran to Jesus and flung herself at him. 'I see they know each other,' I couldn't help thinking. She knelt there sobbing, and, shameful as it is, she started kissing his feet! In my house! And it got worse. She had perfume with her, and this she poured over his feet; she knelt massaging the oil into his skin, weeping and using her own hair to wipe up the excess. Well, this is a household where no such scandalous behaviour is tolerated, and I said so.

But Jesus seemed to think it was perfectly acceptable. While she carried on, with me glowering and wondering whether there was a precedent for throwing guests out, Jesus looked at me. He looked right into my eyes, a kind of searching, deep gaze, as though he wanted to read my mind. It made me feel uncomfortable And I struggled to meet his gaze. Then he asked me a question, a very simple one, as though putting a problem to a child in school: two debtors, one with a massive debt, one with a small one, both let off. Which one is most grateful? *'The one with a bigger debt but ...'* I replied, and stopped. Suddenly I knew what was coming next and I felt humbled. There she was, washing his feet with her tears, full of remorse, full of gratitude to this travelling preacher for whatever he had said to her, and there was I, wrapped up in my own righteousness and purity, stubbornly withholding courtesies from a guest and not listening to him, but trying to make him see things my way. The arrogance I had believed to be in him was my own. I am not so proud that I can't look at my own faults.

Jesus leaned over and spoke quietly to the woman, and she nodded, glanced up at him and left. I wasn't going to start massaging his feet, but I did see Jesus in a different light then. In that moment I felt honoured to have him in my house. He changed the way I saw myself. He was a wise man of God.

Other debates with Pharisees on true religion

Luke 11:37–41 Jesus dines at a Pharisee's house and is criticised for not washing.
Luke 14:1–14 Jesus goes to eat with Pharisees, and talks about humility and hospitality.

Other times when Jesus is anointed by a woman

Mark 14:3–9 Anointing on head at Bethany by unnamed woman in house of Simon the Leper.
John 12:1–8 Meal at Lazarus's house; Mary anoints his feet.

Jesus disturbs Peter's household

Mark 1:29–34

I was Simon's wife, or Peter as he liked to be called. Well, I suppose I still am, although after he left I became much more a person in my own right really. It's not easy coping with a family as a single parent; you have to become strong very quickly for the sake of the children. This story is from the time he was still living at home though, before my world turned upside down, and the only worry I had was about my mother, who was feverish and growing weaker every day. I was afraid for her, and my fussing communicated that fear I suppose. Once you go down with a fever, here, it can go either way. Either your body fights it and you survive, or it drains you and you die. She was elderly and frail, and she didn't stand much chance – really we were just waiting for her to fade away. Well, Simon had been to the synagogue as usual on the Sabbath, along with his brother Andrew who lived with us too, and some friends, including Jesus, who had been lodging with two other brothers in the same trade, James and John. Jesus had arrived in the area recently, and had somehow got talking to Simon and his friends while they were about their work, cleaning the fishing nets. I think they had met each other before somewhere – at least, when they arrived here in Capernaum it was as though they were all long-lost friends.

So, after the synagogue service they all came to our house for a meal. That was a lot of mouths to feed, which threw me a bit, as I had spent the morning caring for my mother. But some neighbours rallied round with extra bread and there was fish to eat of course, and guests are always welcome. But as I was serving up the meal, Simon asked after mother. Jesus heard, got up and asked to see her. I wasn't sure whether she would want strange men visiting her, but I took him anyway, and he knelt down next to her bed and took her hand. I liked him for that. I wondered whether he was thinking about his own mother. Whether she was alive or dead, I didn't know. Sons love their mothers here, and there was something about the way Jesus took her hand that seemed to reflect that love. She sat up to look at him, their eyes met, they held each other's gaze, and she smiled. It was as simple as that, but she was suddenly well; she got up and bustled off to help with serving the meal. I don't understand what happened there. I don't know if she saw in him some gentleness that she never saw in Simon, or some sense of peace that she needed, some demonstration that she was cherished by somebody, but whatever it was, it healed her. News spreads fast, and by evening there were plenty of people at the door, wanting Jesus to touch them too, to heal their aches and pains. He was kind to them and patient; I liked that in him. Just as well really, because it helped me to forgive him for taking Simon away.

After that day when Jesus came to my house, things were never the same again, because the next morning Simon and Andrew were up at dawn and off to look for him, and I didn't see Simon again for weeks. Then one day they all turned up again, wanting food, and after them came a whole crowd of people, all trying to get into the house – and it's not a very big house. Well, I felt like asking him where he thought the food was going to come from, since he hadn't been out fishing for weeks, but somehow my neighbours helped me out. I'd be lost without the community here, never mind Simon. Well, there they were, hanging on Jesus's every word, and they didn't notice some men going up onto the roof. I saw them and I tried to stop them – I'd got fish drying up there – but they went up anyway and next thing I knew they were making a hole in the roof! They lowered a friend down on a stretcher, right in front of Jesus! I missed what happened next because I was so put out about the roof. Who was going to fix it? In that moment I wished Jesus was not in my house, I have to admit. He was demanding, he brought bother and hassle, he was a disturbance and a nuisance, and he was stopping my husband earning a living to keep us all off the streets. But Jesus had a way of looking at you and you'd melt inside. I didn't know where to put myself sometimes. It was as though he was saying, 'I'm sorry, I know this is hard for you, but it has to be …' It was Simon's place to say that, but he never did; it was Jesus who communicated to me his sympathy and compassion.

But still he took Simon away. From then on I saw Simon sometimes, but he never came back to live with me again properly. The men talk about the sacrifices they made to follow Jesus, but I made a sacrifice too. I never complained and I never got in his way; I coped and I held the household together; I wept and I struggled – all because of this man who had healed my mother. Although I have sometimes felt angry, deep down I know it could not have been any other way. I didn't go and follow, I stayed put and let Simon follow. Jesus valued that, I think, even if Simon never did.

Other healings

Mark 2:1 Jesus 'at home', cures a paralysed man.

Mark 5:22–43 Jairus brings Jesus to his home to heal his daughter.

Mark 7:24–30 Jesus is in someone's house in secret, in Tyre, and is confronted by a Syro-Phoenician woman who wants him to heal her daughter.

Jesus in the home of Lazarus, Martha and Mary

Luke 10:38–42

I am Lazarus. I never married, I never wanted to. I don't know if it was because women to me were sisters, and that I had learned not to see them with desire, or if that was simply my way. But I never married. At the time of the story I am telling you, I lived with my sisters, Martha and Mary. They were not married either; our parents had died before arrangements for marriage were made, and somehow time had passed and we were all still together; it didn't seem to matter that much. On this particular day we were excited because Jesus was coming. I had met Jesus some years before. He had travelled down to the wilderness of Judea to hear John the Baptist preach, and I was there too. We just liked each other; he came home with me for a break from the desert and met my sisters, and it was as though he was part of the family. He could have married either of them, but he didn't seem to have marriage on his mind; he was all fired up with talk of the Kingdom, God's kingdom, full of energy. I loved to be with him, to be carried away by the ideas he was putting together, to be there to encourage him and debate with him, to sit in his warmth, his charisma, full of love and humour. We would stay up long into the night, glowing with the sense that something powerful was going to happen soon, and we grew very close. Sometimes we didn't need to talk any more – our eyes would meet, and that gaze held more depth and more meaning than a thousand words. I felt that I wanted to drink in his whole soul and know him completely, so precious was he, so glad of my company but always ahead of me, his thinking always beyond mine, his heart gentler, his courage stronger, his spirit greater. He was altogether a greater soul than I; always I treasured his love for me, but never really felt I had given back enough in return. He left in the end. He said he felt he needed to be baptised by John, and then he started his public preaching, so I didn't see much of him. Today, then, we were excited that he was coming home.

In he came, with his disciples; they were all welcome of course, but I confess to a twinge of resentment. These men who followed him round all the time, his students, I was sure they didn't have the same understanding of him that I had, and I didn't want them to have, either. I wished I could join their group, but then who would earn the money to keep Mary and Martha? I felt my responsibility to them very strongly since we had no parents; I wasn't prepared to leave them unless I knew they were going to be secure. Certainly they could earn a bit for themselves, but not enough to be safe. I loved my sisters. The disciples sometimes boasted that they had left their families to follow Jesus, as though that made them extra holy in the sight of God, but Jesus had never asked me to follow him – he knew I belonged here. And now here he was honouring us with a visit, affirming that it was fine for us to be living here together, not tramping round the country with him. It turned out that I did join the group towards the end, or towards the beginning, depending on how you look at it, but that's another story. He came to stay with me – with us – in his last days. It seemed to me that he was glad of our company. He wanted to be close, to feel loved in a simple and easy way without all the questions his disciples constantly asked him. It was as though we needed to be near each other then. We were his family, his beloved.

Well anyway, that was all in the future at this point. Jesus had come to see us, and we were all overjoyed. I brought him in, embraced him; it was so good to feel his energy and love again. We sat down together, the disciples too, and Mary came to join us. Mary is a listener. She was close to Jesus in her own way; I think she would have married him, had he asked, but he never did. She sat on the floor with the men and gazed at him, rocking slightly as she listened. And he talked. He made us laugh, he made us feel close, he invoked a sense of the presence of God, he shared his energy and his inspiration with us and we loved him. I loved him. Then in burst Martha, her arms full of kindling for the oven, and as though nobody else was there. She threw the kindling on the floor, glared at Mary, and started shouting at Jesus! Typical Martha, she always says exactly what she thinks, but the disciples stared in astonishment. How did she dare speak to the teacher like that? Their faces were a picture! *When exactly was someone going to show some consideration to her, and send Mary back to help with the meal? They'd got things to do, both of them, they'd been planning this meal for days and Mary knew it. Where was the bread? Who was mixing the wine?* She was furious. She stopped. There was silence. Peter moved as though about to have a go at her. He didn't much like women speaking to Jesus at the best of times. But Jesus looked at him, his eyes sparkling. *'These people can wait for their food, Martha; you come and sit with us. Mary's right.'* And he gestured to the disciples to make room for her on the mat, and carried on from where he'd left off. We ate late that night, and everyone was very polite to Martha about the catering.

Other teaching

Mark 9:33–37 Jesus in house in Capernaum, teaching on greatness.

Affirming our own sacred space: Holy Spirit at home

When Paul says in 1 Corinthians 3:16, *'Do you not know that you are God's temple and that God's spirit dwells in you?'* I think of a tipi. The Native Americans of the plains traditionally used the tipi as a home but it is also in itself a sacred symbol expressing the human relationship with God, Wakan Tanka or *Great Mysterious*. Home consists simply of a frame and covering in the traditional form, which in itself represents the sky, and the ground the earth. The poles represent the straight path humanity can take in journeying to God. There is a smoke hole at the top and a fire at the centre. The fire represents the presence of God within a person, or in a wider sense God within the world and the universe; the smoke hole is the way by which a person can find spiritual liberation, oneness with God, who is as much beyond the tipi as within it. The community living together would be made up of several tipis in a circle, sometimes facing inwards, sometimes facing east and the rising sun, and at other times in response to prevailing wind and weather. A tipi is moveable (a wigwam, incidentally, is a fixed structure, a quite different concept); the name means 'something for living in'.

The beautiful simplicity of a family living space that is at once spiritual symbol and a way of dwelling in harmony with the environment is surely the purest expression of what home can be. Everything else is a complication. We, in our homes, can draw from that profound intention. Let us look at the things around us with the same depth of insight. Let us contemplate the gospel accounts of Jesus entering people's homes as stories of Christ within; the effect that the presence of Christ within us can have. Suddenly the ordinary is transformed into a vehicle for contemplation and insight. (It is interesting to note, by the way, that there is some similarity between the spiritual significance of the tipi and the ancient Chinese understanding of spiritual energy, *Chi*, which is represented by a symbol depicting a pot of water over a fire. This fire and water is located within the human belly. We house spiritual power, which creates change or reaction in us, as fire evaporates water.)

Below are a number of contemplations which play with the idea of opening the doors and windows in our minds, the ones we shut when we decide to live entirely in the material world, relying only on our own intellect, hard facts and our capacity for reason. Living an entirely material life makes no sense to the world view of most cultures who live alongside us and who have preceded us. It's like denying the fire at the centre of the tipi. Over the last few centuries we have taken a pride in our capacity to debate the existence of God, but reasoning does not bring God-fire into our lives (or eliminate God either), any more than learning to read music opens our voice to song. It can help us develop and move on, but it is not enough on its own. It is surely better to sing without knowing anything about reading music, than to know everything about reading music but never sing. To experience a rhythm at its deepest you have to play it yourself. To know a dance you have to dance it, to understand the water you have to swim in it, sail on it, surf it … to learn to ride a bike, you have to do a lot more than read a book about it. And the same with God. We are used to talking about God as a kind of super-person (which is very anthropocentric of us …) but what about God as *environment*? What about God as *experience*? What about God the Dance, instead of Lord *of* the Dance? Or God our Song, God the Air, God the Life, God the Rhythm of the Drum, God the Ecstasy of shared prayer between soul-lovers? *God in whom we live and move and have our being* (Acts 17:28). *The Lord is my strength and my song* (Exodus 15:2, Psalm 118:14, Isaiah 12:2).

We limit God by our language, but God is limitless. We kid ourselves that we know God because we can talk to each other about God, using words like 'love', and 'Father', and 'Holy'. We forget that these are just labels and we each have a different understanding of them. We say we are going to church to pray to God – but God is with us all the time, in our own homes and in our everyday lives. Our daily routines are our devotions; God reads the heart.

Letting God in is only meaningful if as a result we live our ordinary lives in an increasingly loving way. Jesus's teaching was that living in the presence of God means communicating God's love to all we encounter. Just feeling good inside is not enough. Just being nice to one another is not enough either. Welcoming the God of love only has meaning if in addition to knowing that love within ourselves we also share it with others, indiscriminately, boldly, courageously, defiantly and outrageously – a city on a hill, a lamp on a lamp stand, and not a light hidden under a bucket.

Sacred space is where we experience communication from God. Potentially, anywhere can be sacred space, if we find meaning there. Above, I described how the tipi has a symbolic value. In the Bible we read how the furniture and design of the tabernacle, and later the temple, also has great meaning. House of God is house of prayer. Surely the converse is also true: house of prayer is house of God. The house, traditionally the preserve of women in biblical and other cultures, is not just a secular space in which secular activities take place; it is, like the tipi, a centre of loving, of storytelling, of living out the reality of God's word in daily life. The home is where, for many, daily life unfolds; the routines, the tasks, the functions of the different rooms, all can play a part in daily contemplation. By spending time in the house the occupant is not shut off from the spiritual life, but living it; the home is where the reality of spiritual life is lived out, a microcosm of the wider world. Here, then, is an opportunity to reflect on things and places around the home and how they might become objects or stations of contemplation.

Stations of the home: Kitchen

Jacob was at home where he liked to be, cooking a pot of lentil broth, when his brother Esau came in from the fields. Esau was hungry, and asked his brother for a bowl of the broth, an innocent enough request. But Jacob, seeing his opportunity, said he would only share his food if Esau surrendered his birthright to him, the inheritance of the firstborn son. Esau, his mind on his stomach, carelessly relinquished his legacy to his brother, and the bowl was placed in his hands.

From Genesis 25:29–34

During a drought, Elijah the prophet was told by God to go to Zarephath, where he would find a widow who would feed him. Coming to that village, he saw a woman collecting sticks, and asked her for a drink of water, which she gave. He then asked for bread, but she explained that she had none, that all she had was a handful of meal and a drop of oil, which she was about to cook for herself and her son, and after that she expected them to starve. But Elijah told her not to be afraid, but to give him the bread she made. Amazingly, the widow baked and gave her food not to her precious son, but to this stranger. In return, Elijah blessed her, so that her grain and oil never ran out until the drought was over.

1 Kings 17:8–16

Dives was a rich man, Lazarus a beggar at his gate. Dives did nothing to care for Lazarus, who died and was taken by angels to be with Abraham. Dives too died, and went to Hades, where he begged Lazarus to help him, or at least to visit earth and warn his brothers to change their selfish ways. But his request was refused: 'If they do not listen to Moses and the prophets, neither will they be convinced even if someone rises from the dead.'

Luke 16:19–31 (last line from NRSV)

Reflection

Am I Jacob, so quick to manipulate, to take advantage of weakness, of another's hunger? What I make and give to others, do I give expecting favour in return? Do I give at a price, so that others leave my company feeling they have not gained but lost? Do I ask too much of people, having my own schemes and desires at heart, my own neat idea of the way things should be? I wish my kitchen to be an honest place, a place where goodness abounds in the cooking pots and in the hearts of all who come to share.

Or am I that widow, so worried about the future, waiting resignedly for death to overwhelm her, afraid for her dependants, gripped by poverty? If not materially, then spiritually, am I like her? Yet all she had she gave away in faith. Am I like her, in all honesty? Or am I Dives, wrapped up in the good things of life, comfortably blind to the need at my gates, deaf to the words of the prophets, of the greatest prophet, insensible to the needs of others until I find myself in need, too late? If I am Dives' brother or sister then let me get up from my table, walk down to the gate and give, gladly, from my abundance. I wish my cooking-place be a hub of generosity, a point from which goodness is given out, a place where sharing and kindness come naturally.

Blessing
May the Lord of the hungry come here and find goodness.
Lord of creatures and harvests,
come and find gratitude.
Lord of life,
come in and see bread broken in your memory,
the fruit of the earth shared freely in this, your home,
Amen

Stations of the home: The sitting place

When Jesus was at home, he attracted so many people who wanted his attention, his healing hands and forgiving voice, that the room would be full, crowds blocking the doorways and jostling to get closer. Anyone playing host to him could expect to get nothing done for the duration of his stay – they would be unable to move around their own house! So it was on the day when four friends brought their companion on a stretcher. They knew they had to get into that room where Jesus was sitting, but the only way, because of the crowd, was to inflict criminal damage on the property. We can imagine the home-owner, gesticulating with fury at the sight of the ever-widening hole in his carefully rolled clay and wood ceiling; clumps of crumbling, dried mud and splinters of wood falling down on their heads. It's all very well to say, 'Oh well, roofs were easily enough repaired in those days.' It must surely have been a test of his patience; we can imagine him starting to regret inviting Jesus to be his guest. But yes, the man on the stretcher was healed. It was a miracle and also an affirmation from the teacher that it is right to take drastic steps to help somebody, never mind the material cost and inconvenience. When Jesus is in our sitting place, we have to get our priorities right.

From Mark 2:1–12

Reflection
Into my personal sitting place I welcome those I value, those I trust, those whose company I enjoy. Into my intimate sitting place I bring those who need to talk,

those who have come to listen, those who need something, those who have something to share. Into my comfortable sitting place I invite those who bring news, who have a specific role to play, their work, my needs, my thoughts, my questions. Into my special sitting place do I also welcome Christ? Do I welcome Healer Jesus and the entire disease-ridden crowd he pulls? Infectious diseases, in *my* house? Do I welcome Teacher Jesus and the controversy he instigates? Arguments, even the threat of arrests, under *my* roof? Do I welcome Brother Jesus and the challenges he throws to all who listen? Prostitutes, druggies, drop-outs as *my* guests, eating *my* food? *What will the neighbours think?* Do I welcome Preacher Jesus, offending the establishment, all those important people I had been trying to get on the right side of, offended on *my* premises? They will think I *agree* with him … Do I welcome betrayed, whipped, crucified Jesus, filthy and beaten, bleeding on my carpet? The horror of violent death, of torture, a victim of state brutality, in *my* house? We don't do that in this country, it's not civilised; I'd really rather keep my distance. Do I want to be associated with this man? Surely he is more trouble than he is worth. But to say yes is to welcome also the joyous Jesus of hope, breaking effortlessly into the locked room of his followers, lost in their grief, huddled in fear, yet suddenly interrupted by his newness of being, surprised by his presence with them, there in their sitting place. And more than anything, I would wish to be with them there.

A blessing prayer

Healer Jesus, teacher Jesus, brother Jesus,
let me know what I am taking on
when I say I welcome you here in my sitting place,
here in the heart of my house, as though in my own heart,
and let me welcome you all the same,
knowing that the inconvenience and the public disapproval,
the challenge to my values and the shock of your message
is worth accepting,
for the sake of your indomitable presence in my hours of greatest need.
Amen

Stations of the home: A sleeping place

Once Joseph had a dream, and when he told it to his brothers, they hated him even more.
He said to them, 'Listen to this dream that I have dreamed …'

Genesis 37:5 NRSV

O God, you are my God, I seek you, my soul thirsts for you;
my flesh faints for you, as in a dry and weary land where there is no water.
So I have looked upon you in the sanctuary, beholding your power and glory.
Because your steadfast love is better than life, my lips will praise you.
So I will bless you as long as I live; I will lift up my hands and call on your name.
My soul is satisfied as with a rich feast, and my mouth praises you with joyful lips
when I think of you on my bed, and meditate on you in the watches of the night;
for you have been my help, and in the shadow of your wings I sing for joy.
My soul clings to you; your right hand upholds me.

Psalm 63:1–8

Reflection

I sometimes have very strange dreams, as I am sure most other people do too. Sometimes, it rather feels as though someone is trying to tell me something! Last night, for example, I dreamed that I was staying with friends in a lovely, very big house, rather like one of the old colleges of Cambridge or Oxford. There was a feeling in the air that there was going to be a party. But then I heard that Jesus was there in the house, and guests could go to him. I was really excited; I knew I had questions I wanted to ask. But instead of hurrying to him, I went to my suitcase and started putting on party clothes! Unfortunately this took a long time. I somehow got trapped in my clothes, and while everyone else wandered off to look for him, I was left behind. I woke up at that point, feeling very frustrated with myself. Read into that what you like, but it has to be said that the subconscious, often accessed through dreams, has a wisdom of its own; there is something in the way our minds work that means that every now and then a gem of truth pops up to take us by surprise. In the Bible, dreams were often seen as meaningful communications from God, such as the angelic messages to Joseph, Mary's fiancé. Jacob, in his dream of the ladder, accessed God's glory, and the experience changed his life. Joseph of the multicoloured robe not only had dreams which reflected his own future, but like Daniel he was able to help other people to understand the meaning of their dreams. While our subconscious may for the most part appear deeply confused or troubled, if not bizarre – the impression we might get from looking at the work of surrealist artists such as Salvador Dali for example – there is also the potential for accessing inner wisdom, and even for interpreting this wisdom in a way that is relevant to us. Deep down, we know a great deal about ourselves that we are not always prepared to admit consciously. Dream-time, then, is precious as it not only allows our restless thoughts to be processed, but also gives us a window onto something rather mysterious – sometimes disturbing, sometimes amazing, often fascinating, occasionally wonderful.

Perhaps preparation for sleep, and the creation of a sleeping room, can be done with this openness to revelatory experience in mind. We can make sacred space for meditation, for reflection, for relaxation, for release of anxiety and stress, for bonding, for sharing, and for accessing deep love, peace, joy and even wisdom, so that we can spend time in that place, engaged in these 'deep' activities. The way we prepare the space has to be appropriate to the age and the nature of the person or people who use it: a child's room might have a cosy book-sharing corner for celebration of togetherness and enjoyment; a teenager's room might have mood-enhancing light effects for chilling out; a couple's room might have a specially lovely bed and pictures celebrating and affirming the relationship; a single person might make the focus a sound-system for relaxing music, or a chair as a place for meditation and prayer, a place of connection with others through love. The sleeping place, then, can be a truly sacred space, a place which we devote to the pursuit of the intuitive, mystical, loving, subconscious aspect of spirituality, in many wonderful, life-affirming ways.

Prayer of blessing
Bless O God this space,
dream-time room,
sleep-place,
sacred to your love and grace.
Bless O God this room,
centre of peacefulness,
arena of love played out and precious humour shared,
of life's rich wisdom learned,
muse of night's gently watching moon.
Amen

Stations of the home: A doorway

'Listen! I am standing at the door, knocking; if you hear my voice and open the door, I will come in to you …'
Revelation 3:20 NRSV

'Ask and it will be given you; search, and you will find; knock and the door will be opened to you. For everyone who asks receives, and everyone who searches finds, and for everyone who knocks, the door will be opened.'
Matthew 7:7–8 NRSV

Peter, on escaping from prison, went to the house of John Mark's mother Mary, where friends had gathered. When he knocked at the gate, a servant girl, Rhoda, was so overjoyed that, in her excitement, she ran straight back in to tell everyone, without letting him in!
Acts 12:12–16

Write on your doorpost the command to love God with all your heart, soul and strength.
Deuteronomy 6:4–9

Reflection

Am I that Bethlehem innkeeper, standing at the door, telling some poor, pregnant woman, some being in their hour of most vulnerable need, that there is no room, no help here? Or am I the one who offered a compromise, the corner of a sheep-smelling, oxen-fouled stable – not ideal for birthing, admittedly (not that I'd dream of offering something so demeaning to a wealthy customer …). Or am I Rhoda, so thrilled to hear that it is really you, rushing off to tell everyone, but forgetting to actually let you in? Or am I the one who hears you knocking and merrily opens the door for you to come in and share my life, come what may? Perhaps sometimes all of these. Sometimes I recognise you for sure in the light in someone's eyes. And sometimes I see, instead, somebody wasting my time, somebody with whom I do not wish to associate, somebody uninvited, somebody who frightens me, somebody asking too much of me, for whom I have nothing to give. I decide when to see you, I choose when to ignore you, but you are the one who chooses when to knock, and I pray, Lord, that at least sometimes my response will be right.

Prayer of blessing

Through this doorway
may the welcome steps of Christ come in,
Christ in stranger, Christ in friend,
Christ in giving and Christ in need.
May this doorway
My own heart portray,
Ever open to Christ's call.
Amen

Stations of the home: A window

Daniel was making the other leaders, the satraps under King Darius, jealous; the king, having perceived a 'spirit of excellence' within Daniel, had appointed him above all others. So the satraps conspired to bring down Daniel, using against him the religious faithfulness that was the source of his strength. They knew he prayed three times a day at an open window, facing Jerusalem. So they persuaded the king to make a law forbidding all worship except of the monarch, and thus was Daniel caught. For despite knowing the edict, Daniel continued to kneel at his open window and lift his soul to the God of Jerusalem, three times a day.

Daniel chapter 6

Reflection

Daniel's window looked out over the great city, over the people down below with their noise and bustle, but his opponents must have thought that in his prayer he was surely looking over their heads, beyond the foreign rooftops, beyond the enclosing city wall, over the land of great rivers and fields, deserts and high moun-tains – in his own visionary mind able to escape, able to fly to Jerusalem, home and motherland, and thus in his heart to betray the king. But Daniel's window did after all look out over the city where he lived, and the voices of the people, the sounds of the animals, the smells of the market place must have carried to him as he prayed. Daniel had made a life for himself in that great city, proving his worth, his dignity, holding fast to his own faith when all around him bowed down in ignor-ance and fear. He didn't pine for something different, he didn't defy his captors and cause trouble; he simply lived in integrity, using his ability wisely, remaining true to his own ideals. Perhaps he didn't belong in that place with those people, but it didn't stop him from leading a fulfilling life. Daniel knew his God was with him there, not bound to Jerusalem. He knew his God was there at the window as he knelt, there around him, within him, making himself known to the people of that city, through his own words and deeds.

Prayer of blessing
God of the mountains you were,
to your first followers,
but you took them through desert to a land of hills and fertile plains,
and still you were with them.
You sent them on again from there,
to learn that all the world is holy through your love
though no place holds you,
and every window looks out onto your presence.
Whatever name we give you proves inadequate,
whatever place we hold you to, you show yourself to be beyond
yet also here, immediate,
responsive to our prayer.
Would that I could pray to you
as faithfully as Daniel,
here at my window.
Amen

Stations of the home: A refuse-collection place

Paul spoke of his upbringing and behaviour as a faultless member of the Jewish community, zealous to the point of using his powers to persecute the troublesome sect called Christians, still at that point seen as a schismatic offshoot of Judaism. Having experienced a blinding revelation of Jesus's living presence, and his concern over Paul's cruel activities, Paul came to see his former achievements as 'rubbish', and his former righteousness supplanted by a new reliance on his faith in Jesus's resurrection. He wanted to distance himself from his past, to throw it away and be free.

From Philippians 3:2–11

Reflection

Paul must have been pretty ashamed of himself, persecuting those he later came to realise were right. But that vision gave him a turning point, a point at which he could change, and everybody would understand why. Sometimes I wish I could have that blinding revelation that would allow me to stop in my tracks and become a completely new person, healed, forgiven and supremely confident in the rightness of my new mission. It's not that I have spent my past locking up prisoners of conscience, but there are other things …

   Paul said the things he used to feel good about in his past were 'rubbish'. Like bits of my past, I have a problem with rubbish. I am really bad at throwing things away when it means they will just take up space in a landfill site. I loathe the thought of burying all that debris in the earth: wasted resources, non-degradables, for future generations to find. So I hold on to things in the hope that they will be useful. Recycling bins and charity shops are my conscience-salve; I return from the bottle bank with the same sense of release with which another might return from a confessional box. Memories too, perhaps, can be recycled. Sometimes they can be useful, as lessons, as layers of experience, as sources of anecdote and advice to others, as snippets of pleasure or peace. But sometimes the old stuff really does need clearing out for the sake of the new, not to mention everybody's sanity; what is of no real value must go. Paul let go of his past and knew he had to grasp forgiveness in order to start again. That's what I need to do in my life.

Prayer

Each item that I discard as rubbish, Lord,
I discard with care, for I know at what cost the earth takes my waste,
I know at what cost these resources were made,

used for convenience, then consigned to that mass grave of modern consumerism.
Each item that I can recycle or give away, Lord,
I give with care, with gratitude for the resources at our disposal.
With each item that I release, Lord,
I release something of my past,
some hurt, some worry that has served its purpose
and now sits heavy and functionless,
burdening my soul.
Let Paul's vision of light be my vision,
let his newness and humility be mine,
let Paul's sorrow for the past he could not change, but only leave, be mine too,
and let my rubbish remind me
of his rubbish,
of my own need to let go the old
and start anew.
Amen

Stations of the home: A washing place

David meets Abigail, the intelligent wife of a foolish and arrogant land owner whose flocks David's men have been protecting. Abigail sees the situation for what it is and appeases David. When her husband dies, David sends for her to be his wife, to which she responds, 'Your servant is a slave to wash the feet of the servants of my lord.'

1 Samuel 25:41

In the last supper, according to John, Jesus, whom they called Son of David, takes on this role, stripping to wash the feet of his own disciples.

In John 13:5–14

You desire truth in the inward being;
   therefore teach me wisdom in my secret heart.
Purge me with hyssop, and I shall be clean;
   wash me, and I shall be whiter than snow.

Psalm 52:6–7

Reflection

The teachings of Jesus are clear enough to us, that it is inner purity that is more important and harder to achieve than outer cleanliness. We need to try for purity, that we can stand with a clean conscience before God. Unfortunately we are also reminded by Jesus, and by Paul, that nobody is perfect, we all fall short, and we can only approach God in humility, not self-righteous pride. Cleansing makes us feel better – it demonstrates our intention to try again, to get rid of that which has polluted us – but it is by God's grace that we receive real cleansing, not by means of our own sinlessness.

Prayer
If you cleanse me O God
then I will be clean
but if you accept me
grubby and dishevelled as I am
then I will be happy.
Amen

Concluding activity for affirming sacred space

In the story of Jacob's ladder, Jacob sets up a stone to mark the place where he experiences God in a dream, and calls the place Beth-el, house of God. In the story of Gideon, who rose up as a judge in the time before the kings, to rid the people of oppression by the Midianites, Gideon sets up a stone to mark his experience of angelic visitation and calls it 'Yahweh is peace'. Moses, on encountering God in a burning bush, is told to remove his sandals as he is on holy ground. There is precedent, then, for marking physical space where spiritual encounter is experienced; it is holy ground. The story of Jacob's dream is the first time in the Bible that we hear the idea of house of God. It begins as a place of personal vision and direct revelation from God, not to a particularly holy person, but to someone caught up in the complications of ordinary life – someone who got it wrong sometimes, who misused his power, made mistakes, and acted from selfishness, greed and fear; in other words a real human being, yet one to whom God spoke and promised unending love.

I like the idea of setting up a stone or a natural object as a reminder or a sign. In biblical times these stones were symbolic witnesses. Sometimes trees were used instead, such as the oak tree near Shechem where Jacob buried his people's false gods before going on to worship the true God at Bethel. I have extended the idea into a meditational activity, bringing together objects of symbolic value to mark a particular place. Although I am sharing examples of this with you, it is really something to do yourself in your own way.

Deliberately placing one object or more to remind you of a particular thing can be a very satisfying meditational activity, and something which becomes a focus of conversation and devotion throughout the day. It is not unlike flower arranging. It is also not unlike putting all the family photos on the mantelpiece, or displaying the kids' trophies on a special shelf. It's a reminder, a statement of what you value. You choose things that speak deeply to you. What you create acts as a focus of the wordless language of Spirit, reflecting what you respect, what you hold sacred, but other people may not necessarily notice it at all. I have called it sacred-space blessing, but the words shrine, altar and witness might also appeal to you.

What to do:

- Know where you want to place an arrangement, perhaps because it is a convenient spot, or significant, or will fit well with the room layout. Is it where the dawn light enters a room, or where a rainbow appears in the afternoon? Is it near a door, or a place where something lovely or challenging has happened?
- Have some idea of what you want to express: affirming relationships, celebrating the natural world, exploring the gift of new life, getting to grips with somebody's leaving, respecting the wisdom of another culture, establishing a place where you can meditate each day or pray for people …
- As you go about your daily life be open to things that seem to present themselves to you as appropriate: a feather, a photo, a ring, a postcard from someone, a fir cone, an apple, a candle, a drum …
- As they appear, place the objects that you find where you intend them to be. Then, when you have time, think about how you want to arrange them and why. All you are doing is making a statement to yourself. A feather by a window sounds like freedom. A child's bag of marbles and some felt-tipped pens sounds like a little honouring of childhood playtime. A piece of yew tree (see *Reclaiming the Sealskin*) and a candle near the back door sounds like a meditation on coming to terms with the death of a loved one. There are no rules, there is no meaning other than the one you give through your own contemplation. It's just spiritually-focused still-life.

Here are some examples; then why not give it a go!

1. The smallest one: I set one up a while ago which was a lump of charcoal and a tiny picture of a fish. It was homage to Jesus's resurrection meal with his disciples on the beach, and a hope-expression that a party we were planning would be an opportunity for fellowship and happiness. It sat on the window ledge in the kitchen for ages, and nobody paid any attention to it at all.

2. Eagle centre of light: Sitting on a small table in my hallway, I have a Native American totem carving of an eagle. The eagle represents many things, but in Christianity and in Native American tradition it stands for the soul's prayer lifted up to God in contemplation. It also stands for John the Evangelist, to whom is attributed John's Gospel (see chapter on Eagle). So this is a focus that declares my valuing of the power of contemplative prayer to draw us to God, and my love of John's gospel, but also my respect for the traditions of indigenous cultures.

In front of the eagle is an old, beautifully carved church collection plate, which I picked up in a second-hand shop. It reminds me of the reverence and quiet sanctity of old churches. On this I place my 'offerings'. Beside the plate, I have seven (one for each day of the week, for each colour, each musical note …) simplified cross-shapes which have a vaguely human form, made of salt-dough and painted white. On the other side of the plate are two seal sculptures which were a gift and which represent to me the soul's belonging in God, as a seal belongs in the ocean (read *Reclaiming the Sealskin*!). In the collection plate I might place one or more of the cross-figures, representing a person or people I am holding in my prayers at that time. It basically reminds me to pray for them. I might also place something which represents thanksgiving, or something I am concerned about.

All this takes many words to express, but I take in the information, the meaning, instantly every time I walk past the table. My eye travels over the whole altar with satisfaction and rests on the figures for whom I am concerned; they stand out brightly, reminding me to hold them always in my prayers, but also to communicate with them, to shine for them, to ask after them, to boost their morale, to give them practical help or just a smile across a room. It may be someone in the news or the public eye, in which case I follow the news prayerfully, with them in mind. Sometimes I clean everything or change it, and then I like to let a candle and an incense cone burn for a little while, but I have to be careful with that as the altar is very close to the smoke alarm!

3. Altar of the sanctity of life: Around the fireplace in the sitting area of our house, I have another focus point, which is almost undetectable as such. It encompasses a big mirror which was a wedding present, the mantelpiece, fire and hearth. In the centre of the mantelpiece sits a wonderfully dynamic bronze sculpture of a horse, made by my husband's grandmother. Beside it are wooden carved apples and pears, and on the hearth are fossils, interesting rocks and shells, and a rock-salt candle lamp which glows warmly and was a gift from a good friend. In the alcoves are books which used to belong to my grandfather, including a tiny New Testament which he was given as a teenager, sent off to endure the horror of the First World War. In the back he wrote the countries he was sent to, and the dates. There are also statuettes of Hindu gods and the Buddha, and in the centre I have placed a palm cross.

The mirror tells me I have to look at myself truthfully, and seek to know myself as a child of the earth and of God. It reminds me that God looks not at my face but at my heart. The candle itself is God's presence around and within, shining on and in all life. The natural objects proclaim the ancient, awesome history of life on earth, the wonder and preciousness of our planet. The made objects represent natural things: fruit, a horse … they remind us that our inspiration since prehistory has come from the natural world, the beauty of life as it has evolved. The egg represents new life, the cycles of change and return, of growth, physical, spiritual and emotional. The books remind me of the fragility of life, the vulnerability, the senselessness of violence, the tragedy of war, the fact that each life lost to war is a life beloved of somebody whose own life is broken too by the viciousness of the death. The images of gods and Buddha are there out of respect and affection for the scriptures of other faiths, and my relationships with people of different faiths. There is wisdom and truth in the scriptures of all the great religions, as there is wisdom and truth in life and the earth; we are all united in our mystical love of God and life itself. The palm cross is central because it is my chosen way; I profess allegiance to the king who rode a donkey, the king who refused worldly power, and in defiance of the authorities poured out God's love to the weak and the downtrodden. The whole fireplace area, to me, draws together a wealth of symbols on which I can reflect, and which are central to my own feelings about the meaning of life: its beauty, fragility, pain, light; the requirement of service and reflection of light; the wisdom of other faiths; that which is cyclical and that which evolves and brings change.

4. Focus of world peace and justice: Another focus point I have made is a collection of peace symbols from different cultures, including a dove Christmas decoration, white and red poppies, a rainbow ribbon, prayer beads, an olive wood cross from Palestine … and a picture which I change from time to time, usually of a person, but sometimes of a creature or other living thing which expresses deep need and reminds me I could be trying to do something to meet that need. In this place I keep my Amnesty letter-writing kit and correspondence from charities, pressure groups and the like. It is my small offering of faith in action, but also always a reminder of humility – that I am not perfect and can't hope to be.

Making an altar, then, or a sacred-space blessing, allows the soul to speak without the need for cumbersome words, and can be a healing process. The more you look for and recognise symbols around you, the easier it is to know what to put on your altar. But deciding to make one is the first step; if you do that, inspiration comes! My altars tend to incorporate things from the natural world, but that is the hall-mark of my particular brand of spirituality. Yours might be more people-centred, or you might want to put an open Bible on it, or other more obviously Christian symbols. They don't have to be big and noticeable at all. It can be fun to make little focus points that only you understand or notice. It doesn't matter if other people don't recognise them and put their coffee cups on them. Just enjoy!

Closing prayer

Never-leaving God,
let me be alive to your presence.
As trees sway
and waves curl against shore
in the presence of the wind,
so let me dance laughing with you,
my soul's love.
Amen

Chapter 3

THE COCKEREL

~ Feed my sheep

About this chapter

This chapter takes as its theme the story of Peter's denial of Jesus following the latter's arrest. It looks at our own weaknesses and needs, and those of the people around us. As we go about our lives, these needs affect our moods, our interaction with others, the decisions we make, and our feelings about God. When our needs are particularly strong, we are sometimes tempted to rage against God, to blame God for causing us distress, or to question the Sacred Presence. But God is within and around us, supporting us like water as we make our way through the challenges of coping with life. Although we sometimes feel dragged down by events and circumstances, it does not mean that God is dragged down too. God is the air bubble that brings us back up. God is not always what we expect. In my times of deepest need, I have felt God, like wild laughter, calling *'Now let go and trust me; now come to me, now follow me.'*

In the natural world, a hole will always be filled, if only by air. A hungry creature is not content until it has eaten, a frightened one until it has found reassurance. An unloved, untouched soul will cry inside until it is cherished. We have needs, and we hunger to meet them until they are fulfilled. We look to individuals to meet our needs but time and again we discover that they cannot; in fact, because of their own needs they seem to be doing the opposite – and then comes the blame, the bitterness and the reproach. But loving someone because they fufil our needs is a child–parent mode of relationship. Knowing God is our provider helps us to move into maturity in our dealings with other people. The following is an exploration of need – our own, which is known to God, and the need we see in others, which sometimes we can meet.

The story

Jesus had been saying strange things for a while now – gloomy, depressing thoughts about death. The disciples, Peter especially, had tried to lift him out of his mood and all they got was rebuke. But it had seemed such nonsense: here was their teacher, the most charismatic figure since John the Baptist, more powerful than Elijah and more confident in his theology than Moses, deliberately heading for Jerusalem to meet his destiny. This destiny most of the followers understood to include the coming of the angelic armies, sweeping him to victory and power. God was surely with him, and all this talk of death made no sense. But Jesus wouldn't be shaken; he started seeing everything in terms of his death, even when Mary poured a jar of perfume over him. The disciples said she was just drawing attention to herself, but he said it was an anointing of his body for burial and he thanked her. Then things got ugly. Jesus told his friends he knew one of them was going to give him away. They all started arguing and Peter swore loyalty, but instead of thanking him Jesus gave him a look, saying, 'Before the cock has crowed you will have denied that you know me.'

Then Judas slipped away and fetched the temple guard; maybe he was trying to hasten the divine intervention that had to come. But it didn't come. Instead, Jesus was dragged off, his followers fled in confusion and Peter alone tagged along at a distance, needing to know the end of the story for himself. And so he found himself in the courtyard of the High Priest, warming himself by a charcoal burner, alongside some of the guards who had arrested Jesus. Up came a servant girl, hearing his voice: 'You're a Galilean, you must be one of Jesus's followers.' 'No,' said Peter, 'I don't know the man.'

And then the cockerel crowed, and Peter wept.

Comment

We can imagine Peter – having been up all night, and having steeled himself to follow his master as far as the courtyard of the High Priest – tired, cold and confused, the adrenalin of the arrest gone long ago. Previously so confident of his loyalty, so proud of his name, *The Rock*, Peter now finds, in the face of gossip, that he has lied to save himself. Suddenly the whole weight of his fear, confusion and fickleness bears down on him; he realises he is not the brave man he thought he was, nor does he have the confidence in Jesus's teachings that he professed. What causes his tears? Deep in our hearts we know, for in our weakest moments we too deny our teacher, and worse, we know that he knows. We are weaker than he, we are still chasing our misguided dreams of power, we still hunger for the satisfaction of our own needs, and all too often act because of our fears and weaknesses, rather than out of the irrepressible courage of true love. Why did Peter follow Jesus in the first place? What need in Peter did Jesus seem to meet?

The cockerel merely marks the passage of time, an early form of alarm clock. But Jesus's prophecy loads the crowing on that morning with significance, for it represents the moment when Peter suddenly comes to his senses and realises his weakness, the weakness that Jesus has seen in him and forgiven long ago. There are times when enlightenment comes suddenly, as a rush of gladness and understanding. But there are moments, for all of us, when in a flash of horror we are confronted with our inadequacy. The cockerel is a reminder of our weak side, the aspect of ourselves that in normal life we prefer to smother with layers of bravado, fine words and egotistical self-justification. It exists, and we are forgiven for it. The cockerel, then, is a kind of internal alarm call, waking us to a self-truth that we might prefer to ignore.

Soul friend

Peter is friend of all who reach the depths and see the truth of their own weakness, yet come to realise, however gradually, that they are known and accepted by Christ despite that weakness. That knowledge of acceptance becomes a new, deeper source of strength. Peter is friend of all who feel remorse, who know they have let others down, and have let fears for their own safety come before loyalty and love. Peter is friend to all of us as we approach the truth about ourselves, that none of us is perfect. All of Jesus's followers ran away; who are we to think we are any better? Peter stands with all who have learned humility and self-acceptance the hard way, and become stronger because of it.

Our needs: Guidance

Draw near, O nations, to hear; O peoples, give heed! Let the earth hear, and all that fills it; the world, and all that comes from it.

Isaiah 34:1

Comment

Peter is the one who tries to tell Jesus what to think: 'You won't die, don't be daft! Trust me, I'll stand by you even if nobody else does!' But Peter is talking from his own perspective, his picture of how he wants things to be. He has his own story worked out and he thinks he knows how it should end. But Peter has not been listening to Jesus. One who does listen to Jesus is Mary. She sits at his feet and hears him out. She understands that he is to die, and instead of resisting, clinging on to him, she anoints him, declaring by her act that he is the messiah.

God communicates all the time, in a constant stream of truth and joyous love, but because we can only see our own little part of the picture sometimes it seems very frightening and we say 'No!' in our hearts. That *no* is resistance to guidance. By *no*, we think we are protecting ourselves from disruption, but we are in fact denying ourselves the fullness of life. In folklore, the aspen tree represents listening to the Spirit of God, because of the way its leaves flutter in the wind – they constantly shimmer in the lightest breeze because of the long stalks with which they are attached to the branches. As the wind blows, as the Breath of God whispers, the aspen is there to respond. That is what listening to God is.

Reflection

- Listen to yourself.
- Lay aside your hopes and fears. What is Jesus saying to you?
- What sources of guidance do you accept as divinely inspired? How can you tell the difference between God's wisdom and human wisdom?

Scripture links:

1 Kings 19:11–18 Listening to God … Elijah in the cave finds God in the silence after the raging storm.

Needing guidance, the ancient Israelites could go to the tabernacle with their problems and the priests would consult the sacred stones which God had ordained as indicators of his will. The Book of Hebrews talks about Jesus as our High Priest, the way to draw close to God.

Prayer

Watcher of our ways,
Magnet to our souls,
Ocean to our meandering streams,
Guide to our feet,
Hand-taker and leader of the blind,
do you laugh as you see us stumbling along, or do you cry?
You weeping, laughing, patiently waiting God,
cascading with us down the hillsides of our lives,
bringing your Spirit back to itself,
bring us home,
correct us with a whisper or a shout,
according to our own hearing,
according to our need.
Amen

Our needs: Community

… God is light and in him there is no darkness at all. If we say that we have fellowship with him while we are walking in darkness, we lie and do not do what is true; but if we walk in the light as he himself is in the light, we have fellowship with one another, and the blood of Jesus his Son cleanses us from all sin.

1 John 1:5–7 NRSV

Comment

The term used in the New Testament is *koinonia*, often translated as fellowship, although the Jerusalem Bible prefers the word union for the above passage, and the NEB talks about sharing in the life of God or sharing a common life together. The Oxford English Dictionary offers companionship, friendliness, sharing and community of interest among definitions for the term. Koinonia in its truest sense was what the first followers of Jesus were engaged in during those precious early days after Pentecost, as they shared all things in common (Acts 2:43–47), joyfully, simply, praising God. In its purest sense it might be said to be the way in which Christ returns to earth, for it is the embodiment of all that he lived for. It seems almost a novel idea, to live like this, in our culture of isolated, often fragmented family units geared towards looking after our own interests, with our main contribution to community made through taxation. But unlike most cultures which have spanned history and the world, our society is not typical and not necessarily the best way of being. It is not difficult to look around at other cultures and notice the variety of approaches to interdependence, some restrictive, some liberating in different ways, but often centred around a sense of mutuality. Community is natural. Koinonia is the opposite of what Peter experiences at that moment of despair in the courtyard. There he knows the isolation of being among people who approach the situation from an entirely different perspective, and this fills him with fear for his own safety. Alone among a group who do not know him as *The Rock*, he becomes shifting sand and is ashamed. To be strong, Peter needs community.

Reflection

Peter in the courtyard is adrift, like a kite broken free from a child's hand. Community is an anchor, we the boat; a hand, we the kite; the soil, we the seed. Loving community gives nurture, strength and a sense of rootedness as we grow and bear fruit. Inadequate community gives poor nurture, inadequate support; it can trap us, restrict us, smother us. Individual relationships have a similar effect. But a community is a collection of people who have come together, and the motivation for that union makes a difference to its effectiveness. What do we want? What do we create amongst us? Why do we choose to belong? What balance is there of giving and receiving?

Links

Ecclesiastes 4:9–16 reflects the value people placed then, as now, on the support of friends: 'Two are better than one … if they fall, one will lift up the other; but woe to the one who is alone and falls and does not have another to help.'
Mark 11:17 Jesus quotes Isaiah 56:7: God's house is a house of prayer for all nations. Is it not our role to promote this multicultural fellowship in the name of God?

Prayer

Christ come to be with us,
be our home and our belonging place,
the hearth fire
we come back to,
and the bond that binds us all.
Be the one who holds us all together;
be the reason for our sharing
and the rhythm of our work song,
be our mother and our father,
be the heart of our joined lives.
Amen

Our needs: Forgiveness

Then Peter came and said to him, 'Lord, if another member of the church sins against me, how often should I forgive? As many as seven times?' Jesus said to him, 'Not seven times, but, I tell you, seventy-seven times.'

Matthew 18:21–22

Comment

Perhaps one statement by Jesus that Peter did listen to was about forgiveness. It was Peter after all who directly asked, 'How many times should I forgive my brother? Seven times? Give me a rule, a number to count, a point at which I am allowed to get angry and retaliate …' And the reply, was 'Seventy times seven. You forgive every time.' Judas has no hope, he destroys himself believing that he is beyond forgiveness – but is he? Jesus dies forgiving his killers because they don't know what they are doing. Did Jesus not also forgive Judas? Peter commits a (less extreme) betrayal but does not kill himself. He goes off to find his friends and hides away with them; at some point he tells them what he has done, and he stays with them, and they don't reject him. Furthermore, Peter is not excluded from ministry afterwards. He receives the Holy Spirit along with everyone else and he goes on to become a father of the church. Not only is he forgiven but he allows himself to feel forgiven, by God and by the people he loves. He has learned humility. We too need to accept that, whatever we do, we can be forgiven and have the potential to work for God.

But forgiveness from God is one thing: God is ultimately magnanimous. What about forgiveness from other people? Jesus said we must forgive and forgive, and this is the only way for relationships to survive. A relationship where there is no forgiveness is an unhealed wound. Sometimes we want to wrench ourselves away from people, get our own back on them, defy them because of what we feel they have done to us – and other people feel the same about us. But this is the path of brokenness, of self-destruction and betrayal. Jesus said forgive, and not only do we need to allow ourselves to feel forgiven, we also need to pursue forgiveness of one another with our whole hearts.

Reflection

- Read and contemplate on the instances where Jesus pronounced forgiveness; they are often associated with healing.
- Are there things in your past which still hang over you? What is it that stops you forgiving and feeling forgiven? How *do* you forgive?

Links:

Matthew 6:12–15 Forgiveness in the Lord's prayer, with commentary.

Matthew 12:31 All sins will be forgiven except speaking against the Holy Spirit. What do you think this means? The statement is only in Matthew's gospel; was it an editorial comment, or are these Jesus's words?

Matthew 5:23–24 If you have an argument with someone, settle it before you come to the altar …

Prayer

Hold me Mother God,
and let me know, as a child knows,
that I am accepted still and forgiven;
help me to give the same reassurance
to those who have hurt me
Amen

Our needs: Freedom

For freedom Christ has set us free. Stand firm, therefore, and do not submit again to the yoke of slavery.

Galatians 5:1 NRSV

Comment

Jesus loses his freedom, Peter keeps his. Or do they? Jesus willingly follows his chosen path, dies and finds new life. Peter in running away effects a bid for freedom, but then he is bound in a different way by fear and a sense of failure. No person traps Peter. Even in the courtyard he remains physically free, but it is Jesus under arrest who exercises the greater freedom because, despite circumstances, he continues to choose: silence, defencelessness, forgiveness. Running away from a situation or relationship does not necessarily give us psychological freedom; it might give us huge relief, but relief is not the same as freedom. Jesus in telling Peter about his future speaks in terms of loss of freedom: _'Very truly, I tell you, when you were younger, you used to fasten your own belt and to go wherever you wished. But when you grow old, you will stretch out your hands, and someone else will fasten a belt around you and take you where you do not wish to go.' (He said this to indicate the kind of death by which he would glorify God.) After this he said to him, 'Follow me' (John 21:18–19)._ The freedom that Peter needs is freedom from the fear of death, and when he finds that he becomes a powerful healer and evangelist. What then is freedom, if not the freedom to follow Jesus?

In the New Testament, we read that the apostles were subject to imprisonment and brutality for their beliefs: prisoners of conscience. Jesus in Matthew chapter 25 refers to the visiting of prisoners as an act of kindness; perhaps this was a reference to the Christians of the future who would be persecuted. But we should also spare a thought for the imprisonment of sin, guilt, ignorance, weakness and fear, not to mention being a wage-slave. We too are prisoners, likewise many of those around us, each to a different 'demon'. While we need to address our own enslavement, we also need to have compassion for others around us. We are not told to moralise about those we see imprisoned, we are told to visit them, where they are, in kindness. It is not our place to judge our brothers and sisters but to give them the support that we can see they need, whatever their predicament.

Reflection
- When Paul talked about freedom, did he mean the same kind of freedom as Jesus did?
- What enslaves you? Consumerism? Status? Sexuality? Anxiety? Work? Anger? Do you ever blame another person for your loss of freedom?
- Consider prisoners of conscience, the ordeals of hostages, the road to addiction, debt and crime, the poverty trap, the penal system in this country and elsewhere, the issue of the death penalty in the light of Jesus's teachings ...

Links
John 8:32 The truth will set us free. What is the truth?
Genesis 39:20 The Lord was with Joseph in his imprisonment.
Acts 12:1–11 The imprisonment of Peter.
Acts 16:23–40 The imprisonment of Paul and Silas.

The two accounts above both include astonishing rescues: Peter was brought out by an angel, Paul and Silas were set free by an earthquake. What do you make of these miraculous accounts?

Luke 13:12 Jesus tells a woman that she is loosed or released from her illness. Does this convey anything about Jesus's belief in what caused her illness?

Prayer
Mahatma, Great Soul Jesus,
save me from the temptation

to run away and hide,
enslaved by fear.
Give me courage to choose your way,
and surrender to the rhythm
of the spirit-freedom dance.
Amen

Our needs: Love

Jonathan made David swear again by his love for him; for he loved him as he loved his own life ... Then Jonathan said to David, 'Go in peace, since both of us have sworn in the name of the Lord, saying, "The Lord shall be between me and you ..."'

1 Samuel 20:17 and 42 NRSV

Comment

In Buddhism, there is a word *metta*, which is translated as loving kindness; experience of metta means that others are seen as friends for whom we wish to practise only goodness and kindness. There is a complete absence of self-importance or the desire to appear superior. This, surely, is akin to a blend of two Christian concepts. One is *agape* (Greek) which the Abbot-Smith lexicon of New Testament Greek describes as 'that spiritual bond of love' between people and God, and between one another. The other is *philia*, friendship. Yet the concepts did not begin here: in the Old Testament we have the concept of *hesed* – again, loving kindness – shown by God to the people, and by the people themselves to one another in particularly deep, loyal relationships, sometimes solemnised with a covenantal vow. Jonathan and David were united in hesed, as we read above, likewise Ruth and Naomi. In Jonathan's case, his love for David was at the expense of his inheritance of the throne. This bond infuriated Saul, who called shame on his son, yet Jonathan still put David's safety first and helped him to flee, and they saw each other only once more before Jonathan's tragic death. Peter's failure is that he professes hesed for Jesus: *'I will never leave you ...'* and then his love fails him because his fear is greater. The quotation above describes the love between David and Jonathan. In the gospels, Jesus is the master of hesed, and hesed for Jesus is expressed most powerfully in the Gospel of John, especially through women and through the beloved disciple.

Loving, loyal relationships in the Bible were often formalised with a contract, called a covenant. As with a marriage, there would be certain expectations and agreements on both sides. A covenant of salt referred to a particularly binding relationship. According to tradition it was demonstrated by two parties who each had a pouch of salt. On making the covenant, they would each put a pinch of salt in the other person's pouch, to represent the idea that it would be as difficult to break the agreement as to separate out the grains of salt again. You might like to take salt as a symbol of your own willingness to enter into relationships of loving kindness with all, seeing all as friends, brothers or sisters, for whom you want only the best, without conceit. You might like to use the covenant of salt as an active meditation: Christ, who calls us into the deepest relationship, is there waiting for you with his pouch of salt. But the bond you make is not just between you and Jesus, for Jesus makes a covenant with all. If you enter into covenant with Christ, you enter into covenant with all for whom he died, as their salt and his and yours mingle.

Reflection

- Wherever you are, think of each person, 'She is my grandmother … he is my father … these are my little brothers and sisters … she is my friend …' How does it change your feelings towards the people around you?
- We read that the native peoples of America refer to creatures and plants as brothers or sisters. Apply the same practice to the living things around you. Also contemplate the legends associated with St Francis of Assisi.
- John Ruskin said, 'When love and skill work together, expect a masterpiece.' The masterpiece we are contracted to produce, as Christians, is surely the creation of harmony in the world, a rainbow painting of brother- and sister-hood. What skill do we need, and how can our love grow to achieve this vision?

Links

2 Samuel 1:26 'I am distressed for you, my brother Jonathan … your love to me was wonderful, passing the love of women.' Here we have a very positive portrayal of an intense same-sex relationship, blessed by God, which speaks for itself.

John 13:23, 19:26 and 20:2 and ch. 21 Jesus, who had the capacity to treat all as his family (Matthew 12:50) perhaps had a particularly strong hesed relationship with one beloved disciple, traditionally understood to be John, to the point where, although he had brothers of his own, Jesus on the cross told his mother to see this disciple as her son, and him to see her as his mother, so that he took her into his own house from then on.

John 15:13 Jesus's love was so great that he laid down his life for his friends: Jesus's hesed, his metta, extends to everybody.

John 15:15 'I have called you friends …' Before his death Jesus declared his disciples equal to him in understanding. What relationship do we have with Jesus?

James 2:1–13 Although deep friendships are good, partiality is not. Christianity is not about nepotism. How open do you perceive your Christian group to be in loving outsiders? How much is your ministry to do with showing friendship to the unloved?

Prayer
Loving God,
let me come away with you
to that place of gladness, that time of singing,
to know the truth of your most precious love,
for the satisfaction of my deepest need.
And through my own discovery of delight in you,
may I become as one who can bring others to your healing love,
for by sharing this love, it can only grow.
Amen

Our needs: Healing

Those who are well have no need of a physician, but those who are sick; I have come to call not the righteous but sinners.

Mark 2:17 NRSV

Comment
Jesus often brought people to wholeness by telling them their sins were forgiven: he knew that fear and shame can cripple us physically and emotionally. One of Peter's memories must have been the occasion when he brought Jesus home, early on in his ministry, and Jesus found Peter's mother-in-law there, sick with a fever. Peter must have watched Jesus kneel down beside her, take her hand and bring her healing. He was a witness to the healing power of love. But Peter was one of the fit and strong, and one of the righteous who were seeking the liberation of their people. His relationship with Jesus did not reflect the deep, personal gratitude of a sinner forgiven or of a sick person healed, not until the moment when he denied Jesus and suddenly joined the throng of weak failures, otherwise known as normal people!

Reflection
The sick need a physician, Jesus said, and nobody is so perfect that they do not need one. It does us no good to pretend to be.

Links

Proverbs 12:8 The words of the wise bring healing …

Jeremiah 8:21 '*For the hurt of my poor people I am hurt …*' The pain of watching others suffering hurts us too; it is love that keeps us caring, but what is it that makes us turn our backs? Is it that we can't bear to take in the pain ourselves, or that we have no imagination, or that we think we can do no good, or that there is just too much pain?

Ezekiel 47:12 Those leaves for the healing of the nations, what are they? What do we need them to be, in our modern world? What part can we play in the healing of the nations?

Prayer

Healer Jesus,
you said you had come
for the sick not the well,
the sinners not the righteous.
So let me count myself
amongst the sick and the misguided
that you might come for me too,
in my need for love,
and my need to know forgiveness
and my need to reach out to others
Amen

Our needs: Justice

I will seek the lost, and I will bring back the strayed, and I will bind up the injured, and I will strengthen the weak, but the fat and the strong I will destroy. I will feed them with justice.

Ezekiel 34:16 NRSV

Comment

The Jesus movement grew up at a time of great injustice. Several groups had risen up to try to win freedom from the occupying Roman forces – and this occupation followed other empires: the Persians, the Babylonians, the Assyrians, and before that kings and queens of the land who ruled with a heavy hand. In 1 Samuel we read of a warning about what to expect from kingship: subjugation, exploitation and oppression of the ordinary people, something to which the God of the Hebrews was diametrically opposed. For the God of the Old Testament is a God of justice and has the concerns of the most vulnerable at heart. Peter and his brother Andrew and their fellow disciples knew this and longed for a leader who would liberate Israel and allow it to become a holy nation again, free from exploitation. There were revolutionaries among that band, including people who were prepared to use violence to reach their objective. Justice was very high on their agenda, and the gospels smoulder with their frustration and confusion as, time after time, Jesus the Messiah failed to rise up as the champion of the people. But Jesus was not out to mobilise the nation's latent aggression; he was living out God's true justice, day by day, through subversive acts of healing and love.

Reflection

The scales have long been recognised as a symbol of justice; the Bible makes reference to people who used false weights to cheat customers – Leviticus 19:36 and Deuteronomy 25:13 both have a rule about just weights; in Proverbs we read that such weights are of God. To an ancient people whose currency was often grain, and a measure of grain a day's food, to cheat was to deprive a person of their daily bread. Is there any difference in today's world?

- Justice, *Fíreoin*, was one of the virtues of kings listed in the 8th-century Audacht Morainn. The word is derived from the Irish Gaelic for truth, and relates to the need to find the truth of a situation in order to achieve justice. Do our leaders and the companies who supply our needs exhibit fíreoin? Do we?
- How do we balance our passion for rights and fairness with Jesus's teaching not to judge others? In the context of your life, what judgements do you make and

what battles do you fight for your rights or the rights of others?

- Jesus lived at a time when it was very obvious who the occupying, freedom-robbing power was. The Jesus movement is still living under an oppressive regime, which exploits, saps our labour and dictates the conditions of our lives. What is its name? Consumerism? Materialism? Capitalism? When do we sell out to it? When do we recognise it and choose a different way?

Links

Proverbs 21:3 Justice is better than sacrifice …

Amos 4:1 '*You cows of Bashan who oppress the poor and crush the needy …*' My favourite prophetic rant! Who are the cows of Bashan today? Read the whole book of Amos!

Isaiah 61:1–2 '*The Spirit of the Lord is upon me …*' This is the passage which, according to Luke, Jesus read from at the outset of his ministry. What does the text say about Jesus, his mission, and/or about Luke's beliefs about Jesus?

Prayer

God of the oppressed,
God of the wilderness wanderers,
the marginalised and the exploited,
forgive me my comfortable life,
forgive me my materialism.
Open my closed eyes
to the people who suffer
so my comfort may continue,
and give me courage to notice them,
to speak for them,
to work for true justice and peace.
Amen

Our needs: Nourishment

Your navel is a rounded bowl that never lacks mixed wine,
Your belly is a heap of wheat, encircled with lilies.

Song of Solomon 7:2 NRSV

Comment

In his autobiography, *An Evil Cradling*, Brian Keenan describes how when he was a hostage his captors on one rare occasion brought some fresh fruit for him to eat. Yet he did not eat it, much to their confusion; he feasted his eyes on it for days and days, until it rotted. He was physically hungry, but he was also starving mentally. Nourishment is certainly a primary physical need, but as Jesus is quoted as saying to his tempter, 'One does not live by bread alone.' We are hungry for whatever we need, emotionally, mentally, physically, spiritually. Hunger is a yearning, a pain deep within, a hole waiting to be filled, and we instinctively do what is needed to fill that gap. The urge can become so strong that our own hunger starts to drive us to terrible lengths: we must be satisfied at all costs, and what we take outweighs what we were missing in the first place. This interplay between hunger and fullness is a root of what is commonly judged as 'wrongdoing'. In ourselves we want our weaknesses to be understood and forgiven. But in others we have to look with similarly compassionate eyes.

Reflection

In the language of Bible times it was the belly which was associated with emotion, in the way that Westerners tend to think of the heart. Biblical hearts were more to do with thought and conscience, more like our concept of 'mind'. Where English translations politely say that Jesus was deeply moved, the Greek uses a wonderful verb, *splangidzomai*, which means real gut-wrenching. He felt for people, deep down in the very seat of his being. For Jesus and for other biblical people, the source of compassion and love was the same as the biological source of first nourishment for the embryo from the mother. She gave all that was needed: bodily food, emotional food and spiritual food. We need to rediscover the navel as the centre of our own energy, for its association with the mother is a teaching about the nature of God.

- To feed the physically hungry is one of the tasks of a Christian. But what about feeding the emotionally hungry, the spiritually hungry? How do we recognise them? What can we give? What about our own hunger? To what extent do people use religion to satisfy emotional gaps? Is this what religion should be?

● Meditate on the state of pregnancy, how a woman nourishes the unborn child. Spiritually, what does this teach about our relationship with God? What is the womb? What is the placenta? What happens at birth? How can we reclaim that closeness to God, and the nourishment we once enjoyed?

Links

Deuteronomy 8:2–3 'Remember the long way that the Lord your God has led you these forty years in the wilderness, in order to humble you, testing you to know what was in your heart … he humbled you by letting you hunger, then by feeding you with manna … Read also the account in Numbers 16 of the Hebrews' nourishment with manna. In what sense might God let us hunger, and then feed us with manna? What meaning does this carry? What does manna represent? How does this story relate to the account of Jesus's fasting and temptation for forty days in the wilderness?

Lamentations 4:9 The terrible experience of starvation, written by one who had clearly seen it with his or her own eyes.

Matthew 25:35 By feeding the hungry we feed Jesus.

Luke 1:53 The Magnificat: God has filled the hungry with good things and sent the rich away empty. This is physical hunger and wealth of which Mary sings.

John 21:15 The charge to feed my sheep. Is that our responsibility, or are we the sheep?

Prayer

Let me find again the fountain
of soul-feeding love deep within me
O my Mother,
Amen

Our needs: Security

I tell you, my friends, do not fear those who kill the body, and after that can do nothing more.

Luke 12:4 NRSV

Comment

Peter the Rock – why did Jesus call him that? Is it a compliment, or not? One who is strong, immovable, hard, unyielding, firm, unbreakable … was Jesus being ironic? It's a name that has a kind of security-guard connotation about it, someone we might feel we could be safe with. But Peter's experience demonstrates that ultimately we can rely on no person for our safety, only God.

Jesus outwardly led a very insecure existence: he had no home or money, his friends were unreliable, the authorities and religious leaders rejected him violently because they saw him as a threat; he was a high profile figure in a volatile world. Yet Jesus still demonstrated an unflinching sense of inner security which allowed him to endure all of these things and death. God was his security. In Jesus's thinking there was a distinction between physical threat and threat to the soul. He 'knew' his soul was safe. The verse that follows the one quoted above tells us to fear the one who, having killed, can cast the soul into the place of destruction and horror, Gehenna. Jesus looked beyond the material, seeing everything in terms of the spiritual. To be cast aside and separated from God (the state of Gehenna) was to Jesus the worst plight that one could be in. But although Jesus said that the suffering of the material body is subordinate to the potential suffering of the soul, and he gave the kingdom of heaven pre-eminence over the here and now, he did not treat people as though their bodies did not matter. He made sure the crowds were fed, he healed people, he restored them to life. He did not say 'Oh well, never mind, you'll be all right when you get to heaven.' Whatever his beliefs, in practice Jesus exercised compassion. His security was God, his belief was in the kingdom of heaven, and the consequence of his spiritual security was love in action, restoration to wholeness in the here and now. We might consider our own security. Is God our rock and fortress? If so, how? If not, then what is God to us?

Reflection

- Search the Old Testament scriptures: what gave Jesus his conviction that God was with him, and that the continuation of his soul after death was assured? How do you feel about this belief?
- Who or what makes you feel insecure?

• What does it mean to call God a rock and fortress? (It is interesting to note that the swan maiden's name, Caer – see chapter 7 – means fortress or stronghold, a feminine dimension of security rather than a masculine one, reflective perhaps of the protective mother bird …)

Links

Psalm 40:1–5 'God has set my feet upon a rock and made my steps secure …' For the people of the Hebrew scriptures, the rock is the law, and security lies in obedience to the law. For the people of the Way, the rock is the foundation of Jesus's word, on which we must build if we hope for our structures to be safe. So security is in giving and receiving Christ-like love. That doesn't sound a very secure thing to depend on, but spiritually, in the language of Jesus, it is completely secure. What experiences do you have which confirm for you God's hold on us?

Isaiah 47:8 Isaiah warns against a false sense of security. (The context is a criticism of Babylon, as personified by a luxury-loving princess.)

Prayer

Peace above all earthly peace,
Wisdom beyond all human insight,
Love beyond all love
calm me and quieten me,
that I may hear in the stillness
the whispering of your breath,
for in your arms, Mother Wisdom,
is the peace which I seek
and the calming of all confusion.
Amen

Our needs: Trust

Then Jesus, crying with a loud voice, said, 'Father, into your hands I commend my spirit.'
Having said this, he breathed his last.

Luke 23:46 NRSV

Comment

Jesus told his disciples to trust God in all things. Peter was not ready, at the time of Jesus's arrest, to go with that teaching, and at times, if we are honest, neither are we. It seems to make no sense. What is the good of trusting in something that will not protect its most precious one from brutality and death? Often, our prayer is *'I believe, help my unbelief!'* (Mark 9:24) We go through so much fear, so much pain, and there are times when it seems God is not looking after us as we think God should. But we do not see the bigger picture. We do not know what our individual lives are for; we do not know what lessons we are to learn, what experiences we need to go through, what opportunities we will have for growth, for giving to others. We don't know where we came from nor where we are going. Our ignorance is staggering. Like Job of the Old Testament, we have to admit that we are so small, and the whole is so immense, so awesome, so mysterious, that our own sufferings somehow fit into that bigger picture of humanity, and are held and known by God. The purpose of life is not necessarily what we believe it to be. Work is not what we think it is for. The people we meet are not necessarily who we perceive them to be. Our sufferings are not the personal assaults of a God who does not care. They are something else. Trusting God is about looking for the bigger picture, and accepting the possibility of God's ultimate goodness, reaching far beyond us and deep within us.

Reflection

God's call to trust is not a call to fear but away from fear. This is the heart of the foolishness of faith in Christ which Paul talks about. It seems crazy to go with this immaterial, intangible 'something other' that seems to the world not to exist at all. The call is away from trusting in material wealth, physical strength, even specific human relationships, to depend on Love itself.

Links

3 Maccabees 6:6 In a prayer for help, Eleazar, an elderly priest, recalls the story of Shadrach, Meshach and Abednego: 'The three companions in Babylon who had voluntarily surrendered their lives to the flames so as not to serve vain things, you rescued unharmed ...' They surrendered their lives, but common sense says they might have been wiser to be flexible and toe the line, then they would have avoided the fiery furnace in the first place. When, if ever, might it be appropriate to choose to surrender one's life?

Jeremiah 26:14 Jeremiah speaks out against the behaviour of the people, and they seek to kill him. Standing before the leaders of the city, Jeremiah says that he is in their hands. He acknowledges his complete vulnerability, but continues to speak his message.

Prayer

Into your hands O God
I surrender my spirit;
take me and I will stand
in my own soft, vulnerable nakedness,
and I will embrace defencelessness for you,
and my spirit will dance free,
my laughing spirit one with you,
wild lover of my soul.
Amen

Our needs: Wisdom and peace

You have forsaken the fountain of wisdom.
If you had walked in the way of God,
you would be living in peace forever.

Baruch 3:12–13 NRSV

Comment

The fountain of wisdom is synonymous with the Way of God, and leads to peace. A Being called Wisdom appears in several places in the Old and New Testaments and also in the Apocrypha: Sophia in Greek and Hokmah in Hebrew. Sophia and Hokmah are both female words. Wisdom is invariably given female attributes; she can be seen as a female personification of God. In the centuries before the birth of Jesus the need arose to open up to and explore the feminine aspect of the Divine, in response to the influence of other religions at the time, in particular the Isis cult of Egypt. God, being All, could be described as encompassing the attributes of a female deity. It is a liberating way of expressing the vastness, the all-embracing nature of God, and a lesson in positive use of feminine imagery from which today's church might do well to learn.

From a broader perspective, Wisdom is described in Proverbs and the Wisdom of Solomon as a desirable woman, one to be sought after and cherished. Angus seeks the swan maiden (see chapter 7), Christians seek the kingdom of God, Solomon and the Hebrew mystics sought and seek Sophia. Are the terms synonymous? Perhaps in a way they are: Wisdom's path leads to peace; Jesus's gift to the one who seeks is peace: 'Peace I leave with you, my peace I give to you …'; Angus finds an end to his longing and heartache, which is surely peace. Peace is the consequence of finding Wisdom and the Kingdom of God; peace is the way we need to walk. A path that does not lead to peace is not wise and is not of God: *'But the wisdom from above is first pure, then peaceable, gentle, willing to yield, full of mercy and good fruits, without a trace of partiality or hypocrisy. And a harvest of righteousness is sown in peace for those who make peace.'* (James 3:17–18 NRSV)

Reflection

- What is peace? What is wisdom?
- The people of the Hebrew scriptures, in their love of God, sought to express the all-encompassing greatness of God through both male and female traits, reflecting the truth that in Genesis we read that both men and women are made in the likeness of God. Believers in the early church continued this tradition, until an insidious sexism crept into the theology and all that was female came to be seen as second best. What can we do to restore the balance, and move on from the limited thinking of previous centuries? How can our religious language change to express this limitless goodness?

Links

Exploring the writings about Sophia takes us into the Apocrypha. Although the word 'apocryphal' has come to refer to something of dubious origin, it comes from a Greek word which means 'hidden', and refers to the fact that these writings were reserved for those committed to genuine spiritual study. The books were available to the first Christian community and were most probably known to Jesus and influenced him and/or the gospel writers' records of his life and work. Because they were written in Greek and not Hebrew they eventually received a lower status as scriptural documents, although their content is of tremendous value in shedding light on religious thought around the time of Jesus.

A selection of Wisdom passages

Proverbs 8 Wisdom's gifts and part in creation, pre-existent and lover of humanity.
Wisdom of Solomon (Ap) 7:22–8:8 The nature of Wisdom, and how Solomon prays for wisdom.
Wisdom of Solomon (Ap) 10–11:14 Wisdom's part in history, taking a role normally ascribed to Yahweh: here the close identification suggests that Sophia is Yahweh.
Sirach (Ap) 1 Wisdom is closely identified with God's commandments.
Baruch (Ap) 3:9–4:4 In praise of Wisdom, again identified with the commandments of God.

Prayer

Holy Wisdom,
I put my neck under your yoke
and open my soul to receive your instruction,
that from you I may learn the ways of peace and true holiness
Amen

Concluding prayer on need

Our Father in Heaven,
we need you also to be our mother,
our brother and our sister, here on earth.

Holy is your name,
but we also need you to be the Approachable One,
the One not so high and mighty that we can't talk to you.

May your kingdom come on earth as it is in heaven,
and may we be part of that.
We need to feel we belong.

Give us today our daily bread;
we each hunger, deep in our souls,
and we need you to nourish us in so many ways.

Forgive us our sins;
we need to know we are free
of the burdens we have placed upon ourselves;
we need to claim healing for ourselves,
we need so much to know you accept
even our faults and our weaknesses …

as we forgive those who have sinned against us;
we need to let go the hurts we receive
and break down the barriers,
for how else can we find your peace?

Lead us not into temptation O God;
we need to see clearly what temptation is:
the seductive lure of materialism
and the pitfalls of dishonesty,
the temptation to save ourselves,
and to make pacts with the demons of this age …

but deliver us from evil,
for cold, heartless evil lurks in the shadow corners
where we have denied your love

for the kingdom, the power and the glory are yours;
the kingdom of peace is yours,
the rule of shalom, the sovereignty of love,
and the power is yours,
yours and not ours,
not the governments', not the superpowers';
and the glory is yours too;
may all that we do be for the glory of God.

Amen

Chapter 4

THE EAGLE

~ whatever you do, do all for the glory of God

About this chapter

This chapter is inspired by the Native American association between the eagle and prayer. It uses two forms of prayer: first, the model of traditional Christian intercessory prayer and, second, a style of Celtic prayer immortalised especially but not exclusively in the collection of Hebridean prayers known as the *Carmina Gaedelica*. Both focus on activities we engage in during everyday life.

The story

According to the legends of many lands, the eagle has special qualities. One story which occurs in various forms is that which we find reflected in Isaiah 40:31 and Psalm 103:5, *'so that your youth is renewed like an eagle's …'* The story is that an aged eagle, no longer able to hunt because of the cataracts blinding its eyes, will fly directly towards the sun. As it does so, the sun burns out the cataracts, and the eagle tumbles down to the sea below, there to be refreshed and rejuvenated, its eyesight perfect once again. In Native American lore, the eagle holds a sacred position as messenger, chosen to carry the prayers of the people to God, in a similar way to the Christian tradition (see below).

It is told by many Native American tribes that at the beginning of time, when God made the animal people, he gave them all their own wisdom and languages and he put them on earth as a way of telling humanity about God, and to teach the songs and rituals which would hold sacred truth. The eagle was his favourite, flying higher and seeing further and more clearly than any other bird. And it bears a teaching from God in the way it is painted and formed. As its tail feathers are marked black and white, and as it lays only two eggs, it represents the balance of opposites within the whole: the two sexes, and all pairs and dualities which occur around us. We have two eyes, two feet, we have body and shadow, light and darkness, good and bad, joy and sadness. With our two hands we can work these differences. Often the right hand might lash out; in Native American tradition it is often the hand of aggression. But the left hand, led by the heart, is for gentleness and acts of compassion. Likewise, the right foot might take a person the wrong way, while the left foot will take the path of wisdom and peace. So the eagle became the leader of all the creatures, and the greatest spiritual teacher, and its presence signifies the all-seeing, protective presence of the Creator. An eagle feather – or feathers – is considered an essential component of many sacred rituals, symbolising or invoking the presence of the Great Spirit and the oneness of life. In a similar way, a Christian ceremony will frequently include a lit candle.

Comment

The eagle also features in Christian tradition, being the symbol for the evangelist John, and for the ascension of prayers towards heaven. It is a reminder to us of both our mortality and our spiritual dimension, for we are not 'up there' – the eagle goes up there for us; we are 'down here' on earth, getting on with our lives. But at the same time, we do keep a spiritual connection with God, and in our prayers we can transcend the material and find truth.

Soul friend

Hannah, whose story is told in the first book of Samuel, is a woman of deep faith who pours out her soul in the temple. At first it seems to the elderly priest Eli that she must be drunk, so lost is she in her prayer. But on realising her sincerity he tells her to go in peace, so sure is he that her prayer will be answered. It is her prayer that inspires the words of Mary in Luke's gospel as she comes to terms with the fact that she is to bear God's son. Hannah is special in the Old Testament as a woman who speaks passionately to God and is answered. She, in turn, is faithful in demonstrating her gratitude, though it costs her dearly. She prays for a son, and this son she then dedicates to the service of God as a lifelong priest in the temple.

Prayer in daily life

Intercession in church worship has so much potential as a week-by-week expression of compassion, justice and peace, yet sometimes it becomes simply an expression of corporate concern, with 'Dear God' stuck at the beginning and Amen at the end. Or it is a kind of shopping list of things we want God to do something about, because it's all beyond us. But, at best, it is meant as the prayer of one person or group on behalf of others, or with regard to a particular situation. It is not so much handing something over to God, as though saying, 'If you hadn't already noticed, there's this problem to deal with …' but a bringing of those for whom we pray into a triangular relationship: ourselves, them and God. We are part of the relationship, and by praying we are not abdicating responsibility but making ourselves spokespeople and care-takers for them; we are part of the equation. It is a lifting up of others, an expression of faith, that God's all-seeing love will touch their lives, but it is also about seeing how they touch our lives and we theirs. As such it is very relevant to our daily routines as we come into contact with so many different people and situations.

In contrast, the prayers of the *Carmina Gaedelica* are ordinary working people's prayers, passed on from generation to generation. They are about everyday life, from milking the cow to sailing the sea, and would stay with a family, unchanging, through the years. They tend to follow a threefold pattern, invoking the persons of the Trinity, and they belong to what has come to be called a Celtic tradition of prayer. Those I have written below bring together the two forms of prayer in reflecting on aspects of daily life.

Prayers for children

Parenting, teaching, nursing, healing, child-minding, interacting with other people's children, providing for, entertaining, listening to …

Biblical reflection: In Mark 10:13–16, Jesus welcomed and blessed the little children brought to him, saying '*Whoever does not accept the kingdom of God as a little child will never enter it.*' Jesus also said the meek will inherit the earth. It is today's children and grandchildren who will inherit the earth, but what state will it be in by then?

Remember the little girl whom Jesus valued and brought back to life. Remember the unnamed child Jesus brought before his disciples, when James and John asked for power. Remember the children and their mothers whom the disciples tried to turn away but whom Jesus blessed. Remember the boy who was out of control, whom the disciples could do nothing with, yet Jesus healed him with a prayer. Remember the crowds of people who had been listening to Jesus all day, and who needed a meal, and the boy who brought forward his picnic basket to share. Remember how Jesus broke the bread that the child had offered, and so fed thousands.

God, Mother and Father of us all, I hold before you the children around me, the children in the wider circle of my community, of the nation, of the world. I hold before you the ones who live happy and secure, as yet innocent to the broken earth which they will inherit. I hold before you the ones who know full well what it is to hunger, to live in fear, to suffer, the ones who are already seeing the world at its worst.

I bring to mind those amongst us who lead children astray, who teach them ways which perpetuate harm, excesses of consumerism, carelessness regarding the environment, blindness to the roots of conflict and poverty, lack of compassion for others; those who deliberately harm children, and those who do so unintentionally through lack of imagination, lack of care. For my own part in that abuse I seek forgiveness.

For those who care for children, nourish them and nurture them as they grow into the ones who will become responsible for this your earth, I give thanks. I offer up my part in that care, with all humility.
Amen

Upon each child the peace of God
upon each child the peace of Christ
upon each child the peace of the Holy Spirit.
And the love of life,
the freedom of trust
and the joy of laughter
rest as a blessing upon each little one,
through all the earth.
Amen

Prayers for the infirm

Nursing, acting as a qualified practitioner, making diagnosis, treating, administering first aid, giving companionship, laying on hands, praying with or for the sick, compassionate acknowledgement of emotional hurt, mental illness, special physical needs, counselling, therapy …

Biblical reflection: *The human spirit will endure sickness; but a broken spirit – who can bear?* (Proverbs 18:14 NRSV)
Remember the love of the women, which drove them to Jesus's tomb to tend his body, even after his death. Remember the devotion of Mary Magdalene, who was broken with grief yet found joy, and her love for Jesus, broken by violence yet restored to life. Remember the intensity of love that transforms. Remember the healings of Jesus, full of compassion; remember his obedience to the will of God, that all be restored to wholeness and freedom. Remember the vision of Ezekiel, and the writer of Revelation, of the trees along the sacred river, which grow fruit for food and leaves for the healing of the nations.

O God, I hold before you the ones known to me to be sick, in body, mind or spirit. I hold before you the ones around me, in this community, in the nation and the wider world. I hold before you all the pain, the confusion of suffering, the distress and fear we see and feel. I hold these people up to the light of your love …

I bring to mind those who, deliberately or in ignorance, cause and perpetuate sickness. Those who condone the inadequate living conditions of the world's poor who work as slaves while we live in comfort; those who influence the supply of medical care – one rule for the rich, another for the poor. I bring before you those who ignore the suffering of others, convincing themselves there is nothing they can do, and those who ignore the needs of the people in their own community – too busy, too preoccupied. For my part in that negligence I seek forgiveness.

For all those who offer relief, in this community and the wider world, who reach out in kindness and compassion, to listen and give healing, I give thanks. My own part in that work of healing I offer up in humility.
Amen.

I bring suffering into your presence,
O Christ of compassion,
I hold up to you the pain of your people,
most blessed Christ.
Souls, minds and bodies do I bring
to you our heart's healer,
for you to touch with love,
your hands of grace
to melt all pain with love,
your own torn arms
to hold each dear one close
and bear us through
into the light.
Amen

Prayers for animals

Tending pets, livestock, garden birds, appreciating wildlife, protecting and restoring habitats, dealing with pests, supporting charities that campaign for animal protection, taking an interest in farming, in animal food production, places where creatures are kept in captivity …

Biblical reflection: *The earth is full of your creatures … these all look to you to give them their food in due season …* (from Psalm 104:24–27 NRSV)
Remember how James and John asked for power, and how Jesus told them they must serve if they wished to be great. Remember the first commission of humankind, given in the garden of Eden, to rule the earth. Take up that commission in the spirit of Christ, ruling as the servant king ruled, through humble, loving service, not by violence and exploitation.

I hold before you the creatures that share our world, our brothers and sisters, voiceless and helpless against the ceaseless growth of human power. I hold before you the creatures that live in cages and die in slaughterhouses, slaves to cheap, fast-food markets and people who have forgotten to care where their food comes from. I pray for the ones who die because their habitats are destroyed, or because of the demand for exotic skins and witch-doctor cures, or because they are tortured in the name of scientific research or hunted in the name of sport, or simply neglected, disregarded and devalued.

I hold before you all those who carry out and condone cruelty in its many forms, those who destroy habitats for their own ends or for the satisfaction of others, those who exploit God's creatures, and I seek forgiveness for my own part in that abuse.

I give thanks for all those who practise compassion and gentleness, who respect creatures as God's teachers, who love them for their own beauty and seek to preserve the world in which they live. I offer up my own part in that care with humility.
Amen

In the creatures of earth
lies the beauty of God within;
creatures of water,
radiance of Christ;
creatures of sky,
mystery of the Great Spirit.

> *So Holy Breath of all life,*
> *bring us to our hands and knees*
> *to see the truth of sisterhood and brotherhood*
> *bound in love.*
> *Amen*

Prayers for plants

Gardening, watering houseplants, growing crops, mowing the lawn, harvesting fruit, gathering herbs, arranging flowers, choosing wooden products, managing a woodland, saving a rainforest …

Biblical reflection: 1 Corinthians 3:7 *Neither the one who plants nor the one who waters is anything, but only God who gives the growth.*
Remember Martha, unafraid to use her voice. Remember the driving force of the Holy Spirit that compels us to search out the truth and confront our own weaknesses. Remember John the Baptist, a voice calling for urgent change, tireless in standing up for what was right at the risk of criticism and ridicule. It is time to call for change!

O God, I hold before you the world's forests and woodlands, savannah and sea plants, all the myriad forms which vegetation has taken over the millennia, miraculous synthesis of sunlight and water, primary life without which no animal could ever have come into existence. I give thanks for the beauty and grieve the destruction.

I pray with love for those who destroy, who call for deforestation, the ones who slash and burn. Open the eyes of those who take without giving back, regardless of life in the future. Forgive us, and for my part in the destruction and the pollution I seek forgiveness.

I pray for those who are forced to grow cash crops while unable to feed themselves; those who are under pressure to buy into the trap of genetically modified seed, the fruit of which they are forbidden to sow in the ground; to pollute their own water sources with pesticides; those whose livelihood depends on the success of a harvest and on the market prices of raw materials. I pray for those whose livelihoods are curtailed by the business manoeuvres and monopolies of multinational companies. I pray for all who set up local produce schemes, and who commit themselves to organic farming, the regrowth of precious habitats and fair trade. May we never cease to give thanks nor forget where the food on our table comes from.

For all those who work to preserve and heal the earth and her children I give thanks, and I offer my own part in that work up to you in humility.
Amen

I bathe my soul in sunlight
streaming through green spring leaves;
I gladden my heart in the swaying tall grass
on the hillside
and soothe the tired shell that the world sees of me
in scent of rosemary;
all this and more is yours O God,
all this do I undertake to cherish
and to hold in tenderness,
my own life enfolded in your greater life,
your Spirit in the wind-blown leaves of tree tops,
your Spirit in the rain and sun of life.
Amen

Prayers for carrying a load

Shopping, lifting objects, carrying a briefcase or work-related bag, assisting another with their load, using a mechanical lifting device, feeling the weight of responsibility, of a secret, of a worry

Biblical reflection: Matthew 11:28–30 *Come to me, all you that are weary and are carrying heavy burdens, and I will give you rest. Take my yoke upon you, and learn from me for I am gentle and humble in heart and you will find rest for your souls. For my yoke is easy and my burden is light.* (NRSV)
Remember Jesus who humbled himself, who carried the greatest burden of all, the cross. Remember Simon of Cyrene who stepped forward to share that burden. Remember how Jesus described his yoke as easy, and called people to bring their burdens to him. Remember Mary, Jesus's mother, who carried Christ and met his every need.

O God, I hold before you the burden which others have left us, and which we have increased by our own foolishness, a burden too great for us to bear: to restore the dignity of exploited peoples, to restore lands torn in battle, to give back what has been taken, to end the relentless abuse of our shared environment and realise our duty of care.

For the burdening of others we seek forgiveness and the opening of our eyes to the discomfort we cause by our demands. We seek strength and integrity too, that we may remember the challenge of Jesus, to go the extra mile, to make our service deliberate and generous, even to the embarrassment of those who try to intimidate. May our burdens be made light by the love of Christ, and for our part in the weight added to the shoulders of others may we be forgiven.

Guard us from exploitation and help us discern what loads we should take up and which we can leave alone. We offer up our own part in serving others as they carry their loads. Amen

I bow down to the God who bears me,
I bend my knee to Christ who shoulders my burdens,
I humble myself in the presence of the Spirit who transforms
my heavy heart into a dancing rhythm of joy.

I bow down to the God who lifts me up,
I bend my knee to Christ who enlivens me.

I humble myself in the presence of the Spirit which brings me to newness,
the renewal of spring waking.

I surrender to the God who calls me to obedience,
I surrender to Christ who calls me to follow,
I surrender to the presence of the Spirit which drives me on
into the wilderness in trust and on to peace.
Amen

Prayers for cleaning

Sweeping, mopping, vacuuming, polishing, dusting, washing clothes, cleaning the car,
polishing shoes …

Biblical reflection: *Then it says, 'I will return to my house from which I came.' When it*
comes it finds it empty, swept and put in order … and the last state of that person is worse
than the first.' (From Matthew 12:43–45 NRSV)
Remember the Pharisees, whom Jesus and John the Baptist criticised for the
hypocrisy of their cleanliness rituals, while their hearts remained unloving. Who
are the Pharisees now? Who are the whitewashed tombs, beautiful on the outside
but dead inside? Remember the house in the parable, which was swept so clean
and empty it attracted more demons than ever to live inside. And remember the
woman who wept at Jesus's feet, overwhelmed by her tarnished past, and how with
a word he cleansed her and gave her peace. Remember Martha, so angry to be left
doing all the housework! And remember her sister Mary!

In the name of Love, O God, lead me to cleaning products which work well enough, but
which are gentle to the air, the water and the earth; let my choice as a consumer be
noticed and have impact on supply and production. Let the network of ones who choose
not to pollute in the name of superficial cleanliness ever grow.

I pray with gratitude for those who work to produce non-harmful products and for those
who research ways of cleaning up the earth. Let those who keep our human habitations
clean – the refuse collectors, the street cleaners, the public toilet wipers and sewer sani-
tisers – be given dignity by society. Let superficial desire for cleanliness grow deeper and
manifest itself as a genuine respect for our environment and a longing for the removal of
pollution, wherever we are. Let us redefine our understanding of clean and tidy, so that
genuine purity takes priority.

In times gone by, ritual pollution was seen to separate a person from God. Now, too, the pollution we cause is a stumbling block in our discovery of true love. So cleanse our hearts within us, that we might cleanse our world. Amen

Come O Christ
as my heart I cleanse

Come blessed Jesus
as my soul I sweep clean

Come O Christ
as my mind I wash

with the water of eternity,
the fresh spring water of cleansing,
the holy water of blessing

Amen

Prayers for communicating

Over distance, by letter, telephone, email, video link, signing, signalling, entering into discussion, touch, conversation, eye contact, facial expression, body language, the arts …

Biblical reflection: In 2 Corinthians 3:3, Paul says that the Corinthians are a letter of recommendation for all to see, written with the Holy Spirit on human hearts. Remember how in the Bible God communicated with individuals in their dreams: a ladder joining heaven and earth, a warning, a vision of the future. Remember how the Magi read the message of the stars, and how Jesus read from the prophet Isaiah, telling the people what to expect from his ministry. Remember how Jesus walked from village to village, to speak personally with the people, touching them, sharing their lives, entering into relationship with them. Remember how he was not afraid to talk to anybody, rich or poor, prestigious or ostracised, man or woman, and how he gave the first instruction to spread the news of his resurrection to Mary Magdalene, first communicator of the gospel. Remember Peter – how a cockerel communicated his own failing. Remember how he suddenly knew the truth, and wept with shame. But remember also how this blundering fisherman became the dignified father of the emerging church, his own vision guiding him to go to the Gentiles and speak to them too of Jesus's message.

O God, before a word leaves my mouth or my fingertips, remind me that it will reflect my heart. Give me wisdom to keep silence rather than utter rash words, for by my hasty speech are promises broken, lies incubated and ego inflated, while in silence is peace and in wisely spoken words lies healing.

Remind me, my God, that Christ holds the words of eternal life, and to him should I turn for inspiration and guidance. May his words become my words, and may I learn to communicate Christ's love at all times, with all people, in diverse ways. Let me notice the ones who need to speak and be heard, and guide me each time to the right response. Make me a sensitive listener and a wise speaker, knowing how to bring peace and healing. Let me notice, too, the ones who have lost the will to interact with others; may they be brought gently back into loving relationship. At the times when my faith is on trial, or when I feel intimidated by others, may I speak without fear, strong in the presence of the Holy Spirit. Amen

> *Bright circle of God*
> *encompassing each and all,*
> *angels of God befriending her,*
> *angels of God befriending him,*
> *every child of yours blessed and beloved.*
> *Amen*

Prayers for cooking

Selection and preparation of ingredients, handling utensils, preparing the cooking and eating areas, using sources of heat, planning and synchronising cooking times, using measures, consideration of guests and special diets, and of healthy eating, disposing of waste …

Biblical reflection: John 21 describes how Jesus cooked a meal for his disciples while they were out on the lake fishing. He had bread and fish ready for their breakfast, cooked on a charcoal fire, and he called them to share it. Remember the risen Christ, who brought charcoal and flour to the lakeside and made breakfast for his friends, and how afterwards he told Peter, 'Feed my sheep.' Who is it who must feed the little ones now? Remember the farmers, the sowers and harvesters and animal herders of Jesus's stories, how each carries a message about the nature of the kingdom. May Jesus of the beach barbecue be with you as you prepare your meals!

God of Love, as I prepare each meal, make me fully aware of the ingredients I use: the life within them, their growth and harvesting, the journey they made and the processing, and the people involved at every stage. Let my gratitude never cease that I have food to cook and eat, for myself and those with me – I who am no more worthy than the poor who go hungry. In my abundance may I never become selfish or greedy; bread is made to be broken and shared, and the wine cup is poured out to refresh and unite all. Lead me, then, to food which has been traded fairly, grown with care for the environment and the producers at heart, wholesome food which can be eaten with a clean conscience. When I can, let me give back to the earth the vegetable matter I cannot cook, and let the compost I make enrich life.

As I prepare each meal, remind me that we do not live by bread alone, but need also the spiritual nourishment which comes from you. Let me recall the words of Christ, who spoke of sowing seeds and the growing and harvesting of the grain as analogies of the kingdom that we seek. Amen

Jesus of bread broken,
Jesus of wine poured out,
into our sharing, come,
open our hands to receive.
Christ of bread broken,
Christ of wine poured out,
into our hearts come,
open our hands to share.
Amen

Prayers for dressing and care of clothes

Choosing clothes, making, mending, buying and passing them on to others, getting dressed and undressed, doing the laundry, ironing …

Biblical reflection: 1 Peter 5:5b *And all of you must clothe yourselves with humility in your dealings with one another, for 'God opposes the proud, but gives grace to the humble.'* (NRSV)
Remember the women who followed Jesus and provided for him out of their own means; the garment he wore, which perhaps one of them had made, but which the soldiers gambled for at the foot of the cross. Remember the teachings of Jesus: God clothes the flowers of the field, which are here today and withered tomorrow, so we too can trust God that we will have what we need. Remember John the Baptist, dressed in rough camel hair, distancing himself from the comfort of community life, setting himself apart as a prophet who spoke the truth, unafraid to be different. May the spirit of John be with you as you consider your reasons for dressing as you do, and what you wish to communicate about yourself by your choice.

O God, remind me of the effort involved in producing my clothes, from the production and harvesting of raw materials to the energy-expensive textile industry, and the skills of design and sewing together. Guide me to garments made in places that care for the environment and for the workers, and to retailers who trade fairly. Otherwise, let me never be ashamed to wear the second-hand garments of a brother or sister, nor to give my own for the benefit of others. Let me not be a slave to the fashion industry but instead choose clothing that meets my needs and expresses my own individuality without wasting resources. Bless the organisations which involve themselves in the recycling of clothes, and increase my awareness of those even in my own community who are in need; guide me to situations where I can share what I have with gladness. Amen

Encompass me O God of goodness,
my form to surround,
my being to hold close
in the wrap of your loving.
  Amen

Prayers for eating

Biblical reflection: Luke 1:53: *He has filled the hungry with good things, and sent the rich away empty.* (NRSV)

Remember Dives and Lazarus, in the parable of Jesus; how the rich man went to torment after his life of luxury for ignoring the beggar at his gate, and how the beggar went to paradise. Remember Mary's words of the Magnificat: the poor will be filled with good things, and the rich sent empty away. Remember Christ's concern for the poor and needy, and how he used meals with the rich and disreputable as opportunities to change their hearts: Zaccheus was a new man after dining with Jesus. Remember how Jesus asked to be remembered in the fellowship of mealtime. May your meals be times when Jesus chooses to be there with you. May his spirit be with you.

O God, may I never eat without gratitude in my heart, and the sobering knowledge that while I am well fed, at my gates are starving millions, there because of the economic structures of which I am a part. Let my meal give me the energy to go out into the world and serve, to speak out and highlight injustice, and to reach out to the poor and needy with compassion. Yet remind me too that there is sanctity in sharing meals, and an opportunity to partake of the presence of Christ. In broken bread we celebrate our oneness of body and our love, and our common bond in the fellowship of Christ. Amen

Thanks to you for ever O gentle Christ,
that you bring me to your table,
undeserving though I am.

Praise to you for ever O God of All,
that abundance flows into our hands
that we might learn to share.

Glory to you for ever O Spirit of Love,
that you bring us to togetherness
in breaking of bread.
  Amen

Prayers for exercising

Biblical reflection: *She girds herself with strength, and makes her arms strong …* *Strength and dignity are her clothing, and she laughs at the time to come. (From Proverbs 31:10–31 NRSV)*

Remember how fit Jesus and those who followed him must have been, to walk the miles and miles of rough country roads in sandals, in the baking heat. Remember that ancient wife of Proverbs, who had to be strong and healthy to cope with the demands of her busy life. Remember the point of being in good shape: to be able to enter fully into life and do the things that need doing. May the worthy wife of Proverbs be with you as you maintain your soul-shell!

O God, guide me to take proper care of my body, that it may be fit and ready to do your work and meet my own responsibilities; and may there never be a difference. Keep me from the body-beautiful culture of narcissism and worship of the physically 'perfect', and save me from the temptation to quest after perpetual youth. Keep me also from self-hatred and the impulse to punish and abuse myself for not meeting up to the ideal; may I never make my body a signal to others of my emotional dis-ease. Instead help me to be healthy and strong enough to carry the yoke of Christ. May I be beautiful inside, my troubles and my longings left with you. So too let me perceive the inner worth of all, knowing you see the heart and not the face. Amen

Your strength in my heart,
your beauty in my soul,
your energy in my step O Lord
as I run your race.
Amen

Prayers for making heat and light

Switching on a heater or the radiator boiler, kindling a bonfire or a hearth fire, even turning on the oven or grill … switching on the lights, lighting a candle, using a torch …

Biblical reflection: James 2:14–17 The writer asks us what is the value in uttering a blessing on someone we know to be cold and hungry without actually doing anything to help them. Faith without works is dead. Remember Peter, huddled for warmth by a brazier in the High Priest's courtyard, recognised in the firelight, challenged, frightened. Remember him again, wading eagerly through the sea to the charcoal fire which the risen Jesus had lit, around which the disciples gathered to share breakfast. In Matthew 5:14–16 Jesus tells his disciples that they are the light of the world, in contrast with John 8:12, where he declares himself to be the Light of the World. In Matthew, it is the followers of Jesus who are to shine out for all to see, like a city on a hill. Remember how confused the disciples were by the transfiguration, the vision of Jesus shining with light. What did it mean? Remember the young men in shining white robes who met the women at the empty tomb: *'Why do you seek the living among the dead?'* Remember the lamp which Jesus spoke about, a flaming oil lamp under a basket … how silly! Better to set a lamp on a stand, where it can shine safely and usefully.

For Love's sake, O God, let me never take light and heat for granted. Each time I switch on, remind me of the decision I am making to use energy. Guide me to sources of energy which do not harm the environment and do not present a risk to life. Bless those companies which develop genuinely safe and eco-friendly alternatives to fossil fuels. Let me be aware of those who, because of poverty or lack of communication, have no heat through the cold months; may they be noticed and their needs met. May I be awake to the needs of those around me. May the sight of a real log fire remind me always of the fellowship which fire calls us to enjoy: the warmth and light, shape-changing flames, ancient focus for meal-sharing and story-telling through the night. In the spirit of the hearth-fire, may my warmth and welcome extend to all. Amen

For Love's sake, O God, light up my way, that I might see all with clarity and insight. In confidence may I walk your way, and be as a light and source of comfort to others. Above all let me see myself with the light of truth, in all humility, knowing that you see through the superficial and into my heart, mind and soul. I give thanks for those of all faiths who shine as your lights in the world, inspiring and guiding us towards harmony. Save me from the temptation to burn with my own light of self-glory, and give me wisdom, that I may use my energy wisely in furthering your works of love. Teach me to recognise those who profess enlightenment yet misguide, and those who quietly live a life of insight, from whom I might learn. Amen

Great Light without corruption,
Deep Warmth without harm,
enlighten my heart and enliven my mind,
make my spirit blaze with love for you
and for all that is yours.
Amen

Prayers for locking and unlocking a door

The door to a house or anything else accessed by a key: car ignition, a safe, a padlock, a filing cabinet …

Biblical reflection: *Luke 11:52* Jesus berates the leaders of the day, knowledgeable in cultic law as prescribed by the Old Testament, keen to enforce that law, very wealthy and powerful – and missing the point. He accuses them of taking away the *'key of knowledge'*, neither entering themselves (into knowledge), nor letting others in. Remember the woman who wept at Jesus's feet: was she forgiven so much because of her great love, or was her love great because she was forgiven so much? The true key – the relationship between love, forgiveness, peace and healing – lives on, through history and today, in all Christ-like acts by people of all faiths and none. Remember the love of Jesus as you meet people who need forgiveness, peace and healing, including yourself.

God of Love, let me find your key which unlocks scripture and human hearts alike. Your key is love. Remind me that without love all is empty and meaningless. Give me confidence to clear away all that pollutes the purity of your love, as Jesus drove the money-dealers from your house of prayer. Those who misguide others in the name of religion, who use scripture as a weapon to pursue violence, may they find the key and change. The ones who are at the mercy of such blind guides, controlled by fear, may they too find the key, and win freedom. With your key let us open the door that reveals love to us, a love that works for the good of others, that promotes equality and justice, the sharing of wealth, the feeding of the hungry, the empowering of the downtrodden, the welcoming of the unloved and the unlovely. Amen

O God open me
O God come in to me
O God be welcome within
Amen

Prayers for mending & recycling

Biblical reflection: Mark 2:21 NRSV *No one sews a piece of unshrunk cloth on an old cloak; otherwise, the patch pulls away from it, the new from the old, and a worse tear is made.*

Remember Jesus and his wineskins when you visit the bottle bank, and Jesus patching up his clothes when you mend and reuse items which others might throw away. But remember also the Pharisee and the tax collector that Jesus told about: the Pharisee praying, 'Thank you God that I am righteous, not like this sinner here,' while the tax collector prays, 'God have mercy on me, a sinner.' Let it not become, 'Thank you O God that I am so environmentally and ideologically correct, not like these resource wasters …' May Jesus and the spirit of the penitent tax collector be with you as you recycle your drops in the ocean.

In the name of Love, O God, teach me the way that was common sense to the people of Jesus's day, to conserve resources, understand the properties of materials and mend things instead of throwing them away. There is a time and a place for new things – new skins for new wine, for example! But otherwise, guide me to the same conservation of resources. Whenever I approach the dustbin let my thoughts be for the earth which receives our refuse; forgive me that with each item I consign to the landfill site, I add to the pollution of our world. Forgive us all, for we live in an age of non-biodegradable excess packaging, a monument to our preference for convenience over care. I pray for the manufacturers of these products and the many others which are made not to last indefinitely but to break and be replaced. May they find a more ethical way, yet still maintain their workforces; may employment be found increasingly in recycling industries and clean energy production. Let love of the earth change our priorities, and love for the ones who will come after us influence our behaviour. Jesus's message was that we must change. Amen

God of the air, forgive,
God of the seas, forgive
God of the earth, forgive our abuse
of that which you love.

Christ of the air, renew
Christ of the seas, renew
Christ of the earth, renew
our care for that which you love.

Great Spirit of the air, empower
Great Spirit of the seas, empower
Great Sprit of the earth, empower
us to tread lightly over that which you love.

Amen

Prayers for painting and decorating

Home and garden improvements, creative activities such as painting and DIY, activities concerning the sensory experience provided by your dwelling or other sacred space: lighting effects, scents, choice of colours and furnishings, design of layout …

Biblical reflection: 2 Maccabees 2:29 (Apocrypha) *For as the master builder of a new house must be concerned with the whole construction, while the one who undertakes its painting and decoration has to consider only what is suitable for its adornment, such is my judgement in the case with us.*

Remember Jesus's trade as a carpenter, and how Paul exhorted his flock to work with their hands and earn their own living, each with a craft. Remember the joy with which the Hebrews set about the construction of the tabernacle, choosing from among them people filled with the spirit of creativity, to give of their best for the glory of God.

God of Love, I give thanks for the spirit of creativity, which absorbs our minds and fills our hearts with joy, peace and healing. Teach me to apply my concentration, skill and love to all I make and do, that all may be done for your glory and the enrichment of others, not for my sense of pride. Keep me focused on the task in hand, knowing that you, the master builder, bring all together into a whole work of goodness. Guide me in the work I undertake, that all may be for the good of others, a sharing of talents and a gifting of energy. May we each find our own paths of creativity, ways to explore our inner being and express our deeper feelings; may we each know something of the divine quality of creation, and use our ability as a means of communication. Amen

Spirit of God, breathe in me,
awaken in me the blessed spirit of creativity
alive since the beginning of time,
each new creation your revelation of love
Amen

Prayers for financial transactions

Any exchange of money for goods or services

Biblical reflection: Revelation 3:17 *For you say, 'I am rich, I have prospered, and I need nothing.' You do not realise that you are wretched, pitiable, poor, blind and naked. Therefore I counsel you to buy from me gold refined by fire so that you may be rich …*
Remember how the first Christians shared everything so that nobody had too little or too much, trusting one another for the meeting of their needs; and how the churches grew as those with houses large enough opened them for fellowship, to become centres of light. Remember how Jesus had no money and sent his disciples fishing to pay the tax, and how he relied on a group of women and a network of friends who supported him from their own means as he travelled. Remember how the leaders tried to catch him out, and his answer: give to Caesar what is Caesar's and to God what is God's. Remember Levi, and his decision to walk away from his job in finance, to follow Jesus; and Zaccheus, who dined with him and decided to recompense the people from whom he had taken.

In the name of Love, O God, teach me to get my priorities right. Remind me of the choices available to me. Remind me that the system of mammon demands wage-slaves who will give their souls to earn the money they need to buy the consumables they are told they want. It is a system that asks people to forget the cost to the environment and the needs of others, and to think only of themselves. Give me wisdom to balance the need to earn a living – employed in a way that contributes towards the greater good while providing opportunity for the enrichment of my soul – with the need to gain spiritual wealth.

I pray for those whose choice is negligible, the ones who are caught in the poverty trap, living with constant anxiety and degradation, and the inability to care adequately for themselves and their dependants. I pray for the welfare structures in our society which support and care, and for those who set taxes, that they may be guided to use peoples' contributions wisely and with compassion. I pray for the banks, for the investment structures which flood money into violent, exploitative situations in the name of profit; may eyes be opened to ethical alternatives. I pray for those who renounce wealth and status, devoting their time to your work. And I pray for the wealthy, that they may not find their riches in this life a stumbling block to your kingdom. Amen

My security in you,
my trust in your grace,
my life in your hands,
O living God.

My work for you,
my resources from you,
my wealth in you,
O blessed Christ.

My needs met by you,
my giving blessed by you,
my thanks to you,
O Holy Spirit

Amen

Prayers for travelling

Any form of locomotion, using your own energy, in a fuel-powered vehicle, riding a horse, sailing a boat …

Biblical reflection: Judges 18:5 *Go in peace, the mission you are on is under the eye of the Lord.* (NRSV)

Remember the journeys Mary made, first to visit Elizabeth, mother of John, a journey of solidarity; then later with Joseph to Bethlehem, under obligation. Remember, too, their refugee journey to Egypt, out of necessity. Remember how Jesus walked the country teaching and healing, and his last journey from Capernaum to Jerusalem, towards the cross; then the journey from the Mount of Olives to Golgotha. All on foot, always on foot, except the time he chose a donkey to ride into Jerusalem.

For Love's sake, O God, make me aware of the real environmental cost of each journey I make – the road-building, vehicle production, burned fuel, spilt oil. Let me consider the purpose of my journey, and guide me towards my own best ways of treading lightly on the earth without judging those who have a different way, dictated by their own needs. Forgive us that in our desire to visit loved ones, to see the beauties of the world, to earn a living, to relax for a while, we have little choice but to add to the pollution. Guide our engineers to find cleaner ways of travelling which might become easily available to us. Bless the public transport system, and guide those who plan and maintain it; guide these facilitators of our freedom to understand needs and how best to meet them. Bless those who research alternative sources of fuel for vehicles, and those who choose to walk or cycle. May we learn to change our expectations and priorities. May desirable cars become those that cause the least environmental harm; may we find ways to retreat from working life that do not always involve flying long distances; may more of us find it possible to live near our workplaces. But we thank you that we can travel at all, O God, and that our generation can visit other peoples and lands so easily, and learn the true brother- and sisterhood of all. Watch over us as we travel, and over all whose journeys are driven by love. Amen

As the stream flows to the ocean O God,
may my journeying always be to you,
my end and my beginning.
Amen

Prayers for washing

Taking a bath, a shower, a swim; washing hands/face/feet/hair, cleaning others, washing up, loading and unloading a washing machine or dishwasher …

Biblical reflections for washing self: Psalm 51:6–7,10 NRSV *You desire truth in the inward being; therefore teach me wisdom in my secret heart. Purge me with hyssop, and I shall be clean; wash me, and I will be whiter than snow … Create in me a clean heart O God.*

Matthew 23:25 *Woe to you, scribes and Pharisees, hypocrites! For you clean the outside of the cup and of the plate, but inside they are full of greed and self-indulgence. You blind Pharisee! First clean the inside of the cup!*

Remember how Simon the Pharisee neglected to wash Jesus's feet, yet a woman washed his feet with tears. Remember how Jesus knelt and washed his own disciples' feet. Remember his words of healing, 'Be clean,' and his willingness to ignore the rules about purity and impurity for the sake of human kindness.

O God, guide me to products not tested on animals, that will not cause harm as they wash into the water cycle, that were not produced by people suffering over their work nor by companies which care nothing for the earth. Lead me to products which come in low-tech, biodegradable containers, and which contain nothing that in the taking has diminished the beauty of the earth, harmed life unnecessarily or exploited the ones who gathered it. I give thanks for water, within all life, and without which no life could survive. Remind me of the vastness of the water-cycle of which I am a part, and let me see myself in relationship with all. I give thanks that I have access to clean water in abundance, and pray for those who do not. Let me not forget that there are people in this world who have little, and what they have is dirty, even potentially lethal. Guide me to ways in which I can make a difference. I pray for those who work to clean the seas and rivers, and for those who research harnessing the power of water, wind and sun in energy production. Amen

Come Christ and cleanse me,
all ills wash away,
my heart a bright mirror to you;
shine from me this day.
Amen

Closing meditation

There is a tradition in many faiths that, like the wings of the eagle, smoke or incense carries prayers heavenwards. Biblically, and in the cultures of the Bible lands, burnt sacrifices were considered a way of gaining the attention and favour of the gods or God, the appearance of smoke being non-material and thus of the spiritual dimension. Times change and physical sacrifices today tend not to be ignited as a means of communicating with the Divine, but still we use the symbolic act of making scented smoke rise as though to God. Perhaps, rather than thinking of God as 'up there', we can see the mingling of the smoke into the air as representing the truth expressed by Paul (Acts 17) that in God we live and move and have our being. God is as close as the air we breathe. By using incense or smoke, we can meditate on that closeness of God, the breath of God, as we inhale and exhale. The following is based on Psalm 141.

Light an incense stick, oil burner or some other means to create scented air. You might also like to light a candle representing the presence of God.

Take time to relax physically and mentally, and to be aware of the scented air entering your lungs. Inhale and exhale deeply, calm in the presence of God who is within and around us all. Let movements such as the raising up of your hands flow naturally from the words, and pause at the end to focus again on the breath and the scent of the smoke.

Breath of God I call upon you,
Shekinah I call upon you,
Holy Spirit of God I call upon you;

come quickly to me;
come into me,
envelop me when I call to you.

Let my prayer be as incense before you,
and the lifting up of my hands as an offering of thanks.
Let the thoughts of my mind be as incense before you,
and the lifting of my heart as surrender to you, O God.

Fill me and speak through me, Great Spirit;
touch me with the wisdom of your words.
Restrain my heart from any malice,
and guard me from wandering from your way.

My eyes are turned toward you, O God,
as the moon waits to shine with the light of the sun;
may my heart and soul be tuned to you, O God,
as a musician tunes her instrument to a perfect pitch.

Breath of God I call upon you,
Shekinah I call upon you,
Holy Spirit of God I call upon you;

come quickly to me;
come into me,
envelop me when I call to you.

Amen

Chapter 5

THE PHOENIX

~ Be ready

About this chapter

Ancient minds saw the wheat cycle and the journey of the sun each day as patterns of death and renewal, and incorporated them into their religious observance. Paul uses the same observations to make sense of resurrection: for a seed to bear fruit it must first die and be buried in the ground. The Christian calendar follows the journey of the sun through the year, with solstices and equinoxes marked by holy days; our faith is very much bound up with the natural world's cycles. This chapter goes through the times of day, the days of the week and the seasons, exploring opportunities for contemplation, reflection and prayer in an ongoing cycle.

The story-myth and comment

The story for this chapter is short, but the symbolism is vast. The phoenix is a myth-ical bird that represents the light and journeying of the sun. Mention of it spans many cultures from Arabia to China, but the idea perhaps originated in Egypt. Although details vary, the core of the story is that the phoenix lives for a great span of time – five hundred years, according to the Roman poet Ovid – and when it grows old and tired it builds itself a nest-pyre of aromatic woods and resins such as frankincense and surrenders itself to the flames, from which either it emerges rejuv-enated or a new bird arises to carry the ashes of the old bird to a sacred site. Ovid cites this as the altar at Heliopolis in Egypt. Each culture has its own variation on the myth: the Chinese say that the bird's song is made up of the five notes of the Chinese musical scale (a pentatonic scale); in Egypt, the hieroglyph for the sun was a phoenix, clearly linking the bird with the rising and setting sun. In Christian thinking, the phoenix came to be regarded as a symbol of Christ's dying and rising, and thus it has a legitimate place in contemplation. The phoenix and the grain cycle, then, reflect the natural processes of death and regeneration, the journey through day and night, and the mystery of Christ's death and resurrection.

Soul friend

Jairus's daughter was twelve when she died; she had reached that significant age at which her parents would be starting to think about her marriage. She was no longer quite a child in the eyes of her people, nor yet fully a woman. I have chosen her to be soul friend for this chapter because she experiences something extraordinarily rare – she, and Lazarus, Jesus's friend, and the widow of Nain's son: what it is to die, and to return to life from death. All around her is the commotion of bereavement, the urgency of the little group pressing on Jesus; but until Jesus takes her hand, where is she? What journey has her soul undertaken, what unfathomable rest or nothingness has she entered into? We cannot know. She holds all mystery in her silence, and all we know is that through Jesus's love she came back, phoenix-like, to continue her earthly life.

Contemplations on days, times & seasons
Sunday, the first day: Light

In the beginning … the earth was a formless void and darkness covered the face of the deep … then God said, 'Let there be light'; and there was light. And God saw that the light was good; and God separated the light from the darkness.

From Genesis 1:1–5 NRSV

Comment on the quotation

The opening verses of Genesis offer the reader a dramatic account, laden with dignity and order, revealing God as the origin of all that is good. First and foremost, it is light which originates from God. Interestingly, although it is the light which is declared to be good, God does not allow it to replace the dark that is already there, but causes both to exist in balance; it is the first measure of the passage of time. Furthermore, there is no suggestion that the darkness is bad; it is simply absence of light, a state of nothingness. Of course we now know that day and night are a direct result of the earth's rotation around the sun, but in this creation myth light exists before the physical sun, its source being God. This is echoed in the opening verses of the gospel of John: '… the life was the light of all people. The light shines in the darkness and the darkness did not overcome it' (John 1:4–5), and again, in chapters 8 and 9, where Jesus declares, 'I am the light of the world.'

Relevance

While the sun has been revered throughout history as the source of light and life, the account in Genesis points us away from adoration of the sun itself, and reminds us that there is a greater light that exists independently of the sun and existed before it came into being. It tells us that there is something bigger, better, brighter and older than the thing we think we depend on, and furthermore that this greater light has meaning and purpose, whereas the sun is just a ball of burning gas. It is a call to relationship rather than idolatry: relate to God, who is Light, and who shines on you and within you, the light of truth, self-knowledge, insight, clarity, vision. Relate to God, who makes all meaningful through love, through real relationship. Relate to God. Do not set up any material thing or any person as an object of worship; instead turn to God and be enlightened. Walk in the light of truth. Shine like the moon with God's light.

Links

John 8:12 and John 9:5 Jesus is the light of the world.

Matthew 5:14 Here Jesus tells his followers that they are the light of the world. Do you count yourself as part of that light?

Matthew 5:16 We are told to let our light shine for all to see, and in Matthew 6:22 we are told that if we see clearly we will be filled with light. Jesus elsewhere alludes to spiritual blindness; perhaps here he means spiritual insight.

Ephesians 5:8 'Live as children of light, for the fruit of the light is found in all that is good and right and true …' How does one become a Child of the Light?

Job 33:28–30 In Old Testament times, reflected for example in a number of the psalms, 'seeing the light' was equated with being alive, in comparison with the darkness of burial in 'the pit' of death. This is in sharp contrast with the Christian belief in the heavenly city, bride of Christ, where there is no need for sun or moon, for 'the glory of God is its light' (Revelation 21–22:6).

Points of focus

Make Sunday a day to walk reflectively in the light of truth. What do we set up as our idolatries, the things to which we give homage and in which we trust for our security, that obscure our deeper dependence on God? How does one live a life in which God is truly the source of light, and in which Christ lives as the light of the world? How do we begin to live as the light of the world, a city on a hill? What part does our collective worship play in drawing us together as this city of light? Would outside observers be drawn to the light which emanates from our gatherings, seeking warmth and hospitality? What signals do we give out as individuals and collectively?

A canticle for Sundays

I will live as a child of the light,
for the fruit of the light is in all that is good,
and the fruit of the light is truth and right.
I will live as a child of the light.

I will live as a child of the light, ___ for the fruit of the light is in all that is good, and the fruit of the light is truth and right. I will live as a child of the light. ___

Prayer

Mother of light, surround us with gladness.
Father of light, fill us with bright joy,
that we may build one another up together
to shine out like a city on a hill,
with a light that cannot be hidden or extinguished,
a light that will heal and reveal the truth,
your light for the healing of the nations.
Amen

Monday, the second day:
The clouds in the sky

So God made the dome and separated the waters that were under the dome from the waters that were above the dome. And it was so. God called the dome sky.

Genesis 1:7–8 NRSV

Comment on the quotation

This description, perhaps as much as any in the Old Testament, reminds us that in reading this ancient work we are looking into a pre-scientific culture's way of explaining its ambient reality – through story. In biblical times, it was widely believed that the sky was a great dome above the earth, for that was what it looked like to a people who had no way of knowing the earth to be a sphere. The truth behind this ancient observation of the natural world is in the recognition of the relationship between all forms of water, whether in the clouds or in the oceans – what we now call the water cycle.

Relevance

God willed for there to be life. God's intention from the beginning was to support life. To agricultural people, the weather is of fundamental importance: God or the gods throughout time and in diverse cultures have been held responsible for the sky and weather. The people of the Bible equated unhelpful weather with divine disapproval and prophets such as Elijah made a connection between kingly failure and God's withholding of rain. After their experience of rainless Egypt, the Hebrews considered Canaan a land watered by God himself, such was their awe and respect for the falling rain. If we thought like this, our meteorologists would be our prophets, our holy men and women! They might offer commentary on the news, to determine which of our political leaders had acted against God's laws and brought wrath upon the nation in the form of flood and drought. Although we no longer see the world in this way, we still need prophets who will look critically at the words and actions of our leaders, and challenge them. We still need a way of determining when they or we are defying God's law of love, and a sense of the consequences. Our leaders need to be accountable to God and to the people they claim to serve – 'minister' to. They should be sensitive to the truth that our collective thoughtlessness is in fact changing the climate. We have a power that we do not know how to use responsibly – it is a dangerous situation to be in. So who are the prophets of today, the watchful ones who are alert to God's will? Is that our job?

Links

1 Kings 18 describes a drought attributed to God's displeasure, and the end of the drought, beginning with the sighting of a little cloud 'like a man's hand' over the sea. Is the weather really anything to do with God? What effect do we have on the weather?

Exodus 19:9 & 16 describes Moses's encounter with God, who came to the top of a mountain in a great cloud.

Psalm 68:4 gives God the title 'He who rides upon the clouds'. This is an ancient epithet which was also used by followers of Baal to describe his lordship. Thus, we understand that the psalmist is affirming that it is Yahweh who has supreme power, not Baal, the false god.

Points of focus

Make Monday a day to focus on political activity in the world, for good and ill. What part do you play in global power games? What is Jesus's approach to leadership? What was his mother's feeling about power? What decisions are made on your behalf which affect your global neighbours, the living world, the environment, future life …? Consider your role as a voice crying out, insisting that people in power take notice of God's principles of truth, of justice and mercy, the law of love. How confident is your voice? Watch the news. What is going on? Take an interest in the condition of the atmosphere. Reduce your own pollution of the air. Plant a tree! Sponsor a rainforest! Be aware of the global consequences of our actions, however small they seem.

A canticle for Mondays

Let justice roll like a river,
Christ's love like an ever flowing stream.

(Based on Amos 5:24)

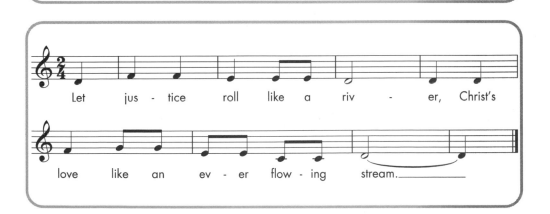

Prayer

All powerful one,
make your presence known to me
in a way I can comprehend;
protect me from turmoil and fear,
from the insidious corruption of worldly power.
Keep me always in the power and light of your being
and teach me to be a protector of those in need,
a protector of this earth in need,
a protector of future generations,
in need even before their birth;
for I am accountable not to those who try to control me,
but to the ones I should serve.
Amen

Tuesday, the third day: Living Earth

God called the dry land Earth, and the waters that were gathered together he called Seas. And God saw that it was good. Then God said, 'Let the earth put forth vegetation' ... And God saw that it was good.

From Genesis 1:9–13 NRSV

Comment on the quotation

It seems it was not enough for God to create bare land and sea on the third day. Having put all systems in place it was as though God was eager to bring life, and life in abundance, as soon as possible. The appearance of dry land out of the sea has parallels with other creation myths from the region. As in the creation of the sky, God is shown to be controlling and manipulating the chaotic waters of the deep. First they were split to make clouds, and now they are moved to make way for land. Sovereignty over the primordial sea was a significant concept in ancient understanding of divinity, expressed for example in Psalm 29: *The Lord sits enthroned over the flood* ... But not only is God ascribed kingship over the powers of chaos: life itself exists through God's will – plant life first, on which all other living things come to depend. It is as though a foundation is being laid in the course of the myth, a structure that will support an apex, the objective of creation – a creature who is commissioned to be supervisor of the whole creation. This is a very anthropocentric view of the universe, and not one to which all cultures subscribe.

Relevance

The creation of vegetation brings together and uses the ingredients of life presented in the previous days' work – light, water and atmospheric gases. This is the first clue, perhaps, to what life on earth is about: growth. Not just physical growth, for we are surely not just physical beings, but spiritual growth, drawing on the light of God for energy. Jesus talked in terms of vines and fruit trees, scattered seeds and fields of ripe wheat. He expressed the spiritual goal of the kingdom of heaven as a tiny seed growing into a large bush; it is not so much a place as a state of growing to maturity, the capacity to bear fruit which nourishes others. Our spiritual development goes nowhere and is meaningless unless it is geared towards nurturing others and spreading new seeds in other people's hearts. Attempts to become 'spiritual' without such a relationship with others are shallow and self-centred. We grow as part of Christ's vine; we grow to bear good fruit for giving, and for engendering new growth.

Links

Genesis 1:29 and 9:3 In the first instance, God gives people plants and their fruit to eat. Only after the flood, at the institution of a new covenant with Noah, does God also give permission to eat meat. What significance, if any, do you think this has? What do you eat? Where does your food come from? How do you make decisions about what to put into your body? How far does the food you eat travel before it reaches your plate? How often do you seek to understand and give thanks for your food's story?

1 Samuel 2:26 and Luke2:40 Here are two children who grew not only in stature but in wisdom and in favour with God. What must one do to grow in favour with God? What does this mean?

Daniel 1:8–21 Four fine young vegans! They are champions of all who choose to eat ethically and in keeping with principles of non-violence, justice and compassion as faith issues.

Points of focus

- Make Tuesday a day to reflect on your own spiritual fruits, and also on the ethics of your physical diet. Are you part of the vine of Jesus, or is your spirituality self-indulgent? The fruits of the Spirit, according to Paul (Gal 5:22) are love, joy, peace, patience, kindness, generosity, faithfulness, gentleness and self-control. Remembering the vision of Ezekiel, echoed in Revelation, our spiritual development is for the good of others, for the healing of the nations.

- Look at the plant life around you. What about the world's habitats? Consider ways in which you can be actively involved in their preservation and/or regeneration. What part do you play in loving all this? In what way do we support deforestation and monocultures, impoverishment of farmers in poorer countries, and misuse and over-farming of land? In what way do we incur huge pollution and transportation costs through what we eat? We belong to the earth – how gently do we treat her? What we do to the earth affects all life, now and in the future, How can we hope to love our neighbour without caring for our world?

A canticle for Tuesdays

My fruit is for the nourishment of all,
and my leaves are for the healing of the nations.

Prayer

God of light and water,
you who dispel the darkness of chaos and confusion,
I give thanks for the beautiful world around me,

for the green covering of living, growing goodness,
so full of your radiant love.
Forgive the damage to your earth O God,
and lead us to healing.
Conquer the chaos of our own minds,
drive back the powers that would engulf us,
redirect us towards the light,
that we might grow with greater strength,
and so be of use to you in the healing of the earth.
Amen

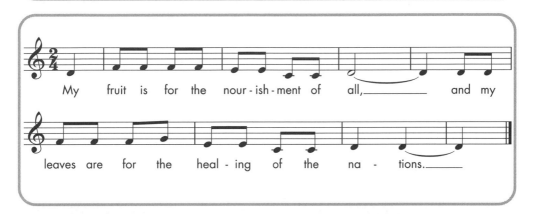

My fruit is for the nour - ish - ment of all,_____ and my
leaves are for the heal - ing of the na - tions._____

Wednesday, the fourth day: Heavenly lights

And God said, 'Let there be lights in the dome of the sky to separate the day from the night;
and let them be for signs and for seasons and for days and years, and let them be lights in
the dome of the sky to give light upon the earth.' … And God saw that it was good.

Genesis 1:14–19 NRSV

Comment on the quotation

This creation story was written during the Babylonian exile. Leading Jews were
brought to Babylon, now part of Iraq, and used for their skills and learning, but in
turn they must also have been influenced by the great foreign culture in which they
found themselves. The Babylonians, for example, had developed a system for cal-
culating the start of each month by observing the phases of the moon, which is still
reflected in lunar calendars today, such as those of Judaism and Islam. They had a
highly developed system of astrology, based on their observations, and this discipline was practised among the educated and members of the royal court, as we see
from the book of Daniel (Daniel 2:27, 4:7, 5:7 & 11). Before this time, Abraham –
himself a resident of the region that was to become part of the Babylonian empire
– grew up in a city apparently dedicated to the worship of the moon. Later, as a
nomad, he would have used the stars to guide him in his journeying. Thus, to the
writer of the creation narrative the heavenly bodies were much more than just
lights in the sky; it was as though they were the means by which God had chosen
to communicate with humanity, to guide and enlighten it, and to reveal the future.

Relevance

Tradition tells us that the Magi followed a star, which to them was a sign. While
many are, with some justification, suspicious of astrology, in biblical times it was
taken very seriously. Thus, the account of God's creation of the stars and moon is
about more than providing light in the dark: it is a way of saying that God set up
systems for communication before humans even appeared on the scene – God
always intended to guide us, both physically and at the level of inner wisdom. But
almost as an acknowledgement that the stars were not enough, the brightest star of
all declared the birth of a new way: the reality of Immanuel, God with us on earth,
Jesus.

Links

Genesis 15:5 God promised Abraham that his descendants would be as numerous
as the stars. For most of the biblical period it seems that people did not live in hope

of a heavenly afterlife but rather were resigned to the idea of *sheol*, a shadowy realm. Life continued through one's descendants, so to be childless was a great sorrow. God's promise to Abraham reassures him in the way that a modern mind might be reassured by the knowledge of continued existence after death.

Daniel 2:27, 4:7, 5:7 & 11 Daniel's insight is greater than that of the court wise men and astrologers, yet rather than studying books, charts and astral movements as they did, Daniel's wisdom came to him through prayer, from God.

Matthew 2 What do you think about this astrological prediction of Christ's birth?

Matthew 1:20 Angels (from Greek *angelos,* meaning messenger) are another way God is said to communicate. There are over three hundred references to angels in the Bible; look them up! What do you make of angels or messengers of God? Can they help you?

Points of focus

Let Wednesday be a day to focus on the real communication and ministry of God's word of love. How can we discern the voice of God, faced as we are with our desires, our hunches, our rational arguments, our limited experience, our inclination to take the easiest option? And how do we interpret the signs that we see? How do we see through situations where good intentions have been hijacked by the god of value for money and short-term solutions? How do we suspend our own cultural ideas about right and wrong, to find the purity of God's message? How do we read the scriptures and bring them to others through the living of our daily lives, in such a way as to communicate our own understanding of the truth? What is the essence of the Word or the Wisdom of God? Peace? Love? Compassion? Justice? All of these?

Canticle for Wednesdays

First sound of the breath of God,
before any star was born,
I sing out God's Wisdom, God's Word,
hidden no longer from Earth.

(From 1 Corinthians 2)

Prayer

God of light,
Speak in ways we will hear,
show us your light in ways we can comprehend,
and help us to respond with wisdom.
Amen

First sound of the breath of God, be-fore an-y star was born, I sing out God's Wis-dom, God's Word, hid-den no long-er from Earth.

Thursday, the fifth day: Creatures of the sea and air

And God said, 'Let the waters bring forth swarms of living creatures, and let birds fly above the earth across the dome of the sky.' … God blessed them, saying, 'Be fruitful and multiply …'

From Genesis 1:20–23 NRSV

Comment on the quotation

In this passage, God creates every water-living creature and every winged bird. Interestingly, insects are not included although many are winged; but also, as any school child who hears the account of the creation is very ready to point out, there is mention of sea monsters – marine reptiles – but no mention of the dinosaurs.

While as land animals they would belong in day six, they were related closely to the birds, and some, it appears, were winged, or at least feathered. This omission, which is of course simply due to the fact that biblical people had no idea about prehistory, creates a monumental stumbling-block for children (and some adults) who are asked to 'believe' the Bible. It highlights two contemporary Christian concerns: First, how should we present our faith to the educated and well-informed thinkers of modern society without compromising what is of key importance to Christianity? And second, what in fact is of key importance to us in our 21st-century faith?

Relevance

The human ability to explore the depths of the sea is a new one, for which we owe a great debt to modern technology. There is vast symbolic meaning in the act of diving deep, and the ocean represents the unfathomable nature of our own spiritual being and subconscious mind. But in the height and breadth and depth of experience represented by the birds and the sea creatures – but especially the diving birds – is the totality of God's presence, the overwhelming, all-embracing Shekinah: *'If I ascend to heaven you are there; if I make my bed in Sheol, you are there; if I take the wings of the morning and settle at the farthest limits of the sea, even there your hand shall lead me and your right hand shall hold me fast ...'* (Psalm 139:8–9) God is not a distant deity sitting far away on a throne like some old king. God is an ocean of love and peace, washing over us, infilling us, supporting and nourishing us. Shekinah is everywhere.

Links

Ezekiel 47, especially verses 9–10 Read the whole passage. What do you think Ezekiel meant? Does it have any relevance today?
Matthew 13:47 In what way could the kingdom of heaven be like a fishing net? How is this related to the disciples' commission to fish for people? (Matthew 4:18)
Luke 5:4–9 Does this miraculous catch of fish have any deeper significance?
Exodus 25:20 There are many references to winged cherubim (plural of cherub) in the Old Testament; they are related to other (female) symbolic winged creatures featuring in the artwork of the ancient Mesopotamian world, and seem to have a protective role, their wings perhaps supporting the invisible throne of God.

Points of focus

Let Thursday be a day to reflect on the spiritual dimension of life in the wider sense of the word – the true depth, the bigger picture – and to accept that the superficial surface existence which we get so caught up in is not the be-all and end-all. Like an iceberg, there is more to each person, each creature, each situation, than we can ever grasp. Find the depth in your own self and express it, explore it, communicate it to others: meditate, paint stream-of-consciousness pictures, dance, write poetry, do yoga, play music, walk in the woods, hug trees, sing, go drumming … Grasp the spiritual dimension of life in the wider sense: the reaching to heaven in genuine prayer, and the diving beneath the surface of our own mind in self-discovery. In so doing lies inner healing. Do it for yourself. Unlock yourself, and see the potential in others too. Be there for others to find their own path to healing. But always allow the gospel of service and compassion to be your motivation.

Canticle for Thursdays

Shekinah, Sophia, Hokmah*, the presence of God is Wisdom.
Shekinah, Shalom, Sala'am*, the presence of God is peace.

* Hokmah is Hebrew for wisdom, sala'am is Arabic for peace.

Prayer

God, spare me from living a superficial life,
bobbing on the surface of the water like a duck
that has forgotten how to dive;
spare me from banality and meaninglessness!
Spare me from captivity, the misery of clipped wings.
God grant my soul freedom to fly ever higher in prayer,
And dive ever deeper into the depths of my being,
to find you, around me and within,
beyond and immediate.
  Amen

She - ki - nah, So - phi - a, Hok - mah,_____ the pres-ence of God__ is Wis - dom.__ She - ki - nah, Sha - lom, Sa - la'am,_____ the pres-ence of God__ is peace.____

Friday, the sixth day: Creatures of the land

And God said, 'Let the earth bring forth living creatures of every kind …' And God saw that it was good. Then God said, 'Let us make humankind in our image, according to our likeness …'

From Genesis 1:24–31 NRSV

Comment on the quotation

It is interesting to note that God seems to be speaking to somebody who shares pre-existence. This may be Wisdom, referred to in Proverbs 8:22–31, or Christ, the Logos or word of God made flesh, described in the opening verses of John's gospel – in some sense, one and the same. Again, perhaps it is the breath of God, Ruah, or the Shekinah, God's presence, which hovered over the waters of the deep. Then again, perhaps the writer saw God as an anthropomorphic deity, sitting on a throne and surrounded by celestial beings like the Ancient of Days in Daniel's vision or in the same way that the other gods of the region held heavenly court. Yet the writer felt that some quality of God was passed on to humans, making them different from other land animals. The word *image* implies that this similarity is superficial: our bodies look like God's body. Yet does God have a body? Is there not something deeper that we share? Having been willed into existence, humans were then bestowed with the task of responsibility for all the earth. We have seen the effects of centuries of exploitative misrule, yet Jesus told us what kingship involves: leadership through loving service.

Relevance

By looking in a mirror should we be able to gain some insight into the nature of God? It seems rather self-celebratory, yet we are reminded that when we look upon other human beings we are to see Christ and to serve them as though we were serving Christ. By the example of saints such as St Francis of Assisi, when we look at other creatures we are also to see our brothers and sisters and to remember that God loves them too. But if we are to hold a mirror to ourselves it needs to be a very special one, *'for the Lord does not see as mortals see; they look on the outward appearance, but the Lord looks on the heart'* (1 Samuel 16:7). As we consider our place amongst the other life-forms of this earth, we need to look at ourselves, at our own hearts. But we will only reflect God if there is love within us for our brothers and sisters and for the earth for which we have such great responsibility.

Links

Exodus 20:4 The Bible abounds in references to graven images and the prohibition on making and worshipping them. This makes biblical culture unusual in the ancient world, as most religions of the time made representations of their gods. Only God can make something holy and blessed with life. Anything we make continues to be inanimate and soulless; thus only God is worthy of adoration.
Psalm 104 All life depends on God's abundant giving, and we are part of that life.
Psalm 74:19–21 Do not deliver the soul of your dove to the wild animals … Have regard for your covenant, for the dark places of the land are full of the haunts of violence. Do not let the downtrodden be put to shame …

Points of focus

Let Friday be a day to reflect on the ways in which you practise your responsibility for the earth and all life through loving service. What is your attitude to other people whom you know to be in need? What is your relationship with other creatures? What is your true role and responsibility as a human being? Where are we all going, together? Where should we be going? Friday is the day on which Christ died, a sobering reminder of the consequences of violence and abuse of power. Who are the victims today of powers who get rid of nuisances, people who speak the truth, and those who do not conform? Who are the ones today in whom we see Christ if we look deep enough? – the homeless, the marginalised, the truth-speakers, the ones who devote themselves to works of compassion and gentleness … What is your place in the world? What is your relationship with other people and thus with God? What is it that Jesus says to your heart? What does *'Follow me'* mean?

Canticle for Fridays

Is not this the fast of the Lord,
to loose the bonds of injustice?
Then shall our light break free like the dawn
and quickly shall come our healing.

(From the Suffering Servant Liturgy)

Prayer

God of the covenant of grace,
preached and sealed by your son our brother,
guide our steps along the path of peace,
that knowing forgiveness in our own hearts
we may enter the shadow places of the world,
speaking peace in the haunts of violence
and restoration to the downtrodden and the needy.
By your love give us strength
to be defenceless,
and courage to raise our hand
not in anger but for healing.
Amen

(From Psalm 74)

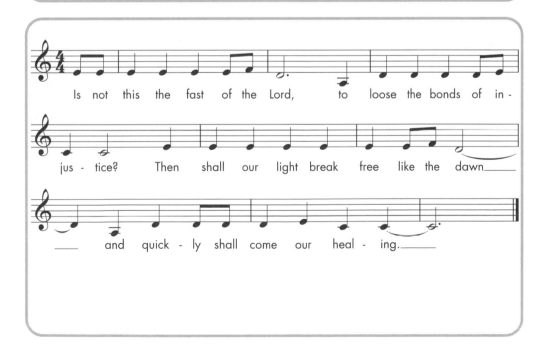

Saturday, the seventh day: Rest

And on the seventh day God finished the work that he had done … So God blessed the seventh day and hallowed it, because on it God rested from all the work that he had done in creation.

Genesis 2:2–3 NRSV

Comment on the quotation

The seventh day, the sabbath in the Jewish world, begins on Friday evening and ends on Saturday evening. Observance of the sabbath as a day of rest is a key feature of Judaism today, as it was in the time of Jesus, and there are many rules governing what one should and should not do. The determining concept in what is prohibited is *melachah,* which generally refers to creative activity involving manipulation of the environment, especially for one's own ends. Melachah is used in the context of the building of the sanctuary in Exodus 31, and rabbis have inferred from this that the activities required in construction are of the type which must stop for the sabbath rest. Any sabbath restriction can be lifted to save life (including animal life), and it is in this spirit that we find Jesus in opposition to over-legalistic interpretation of the law: 'The sabbath was made for humankind, not humankind for the sabbath' (Mark 2:27).

Relevance

In ancient times the idea of a day off was virtually unheard of, especially among the working classes, and even we, with our modern, pressured lifestyles, know how precious free time is; how special a day spent with family and friends, or a day of retreat devoted to bringing our minds and hearts back to God. The Hebrew ban on creativity seems repressive in a culture like ours, where creativity is associated mainly with relaxation. But in biblical times, crafts which we now find pleasurable were undertaken out of necessity, to make what was needed and to earn a living. Creative activity at that time was about productivity and personal gain. It is that from which we are asked to refrain in the spirit of the sabbath, for the sabbath is a day of return to God. The seventh day, then, is a time to draw a distinction between the things we do for ourselves and the things we do for God.

Links

Matthew 12:1–12 This passage contains a number of Jesus's actions and teachings regarding the sabbath. In what sense are these teachings still relevant to Christians who do not observe the sabbath as such?

Mark 16:1 The women felt bound by the Jewish law; they were so keen to visit Jesus's grave yet they only set out as early as their religion allowed, not before. Had they got there earlier, what would they have found?

Isaiah 58, especially verse 13 This passage expresses the spirit rather than the letter of the law. Perhaps it was a passage that particularly inspired Jesus: it is in pursuing our own interests rather than God's that we are criticised.

Hebrews 4:1–12 The implication is that the sabbath is a model for God's true and final rest for all who are obedient – that is, the kingdom of heaven.

Points of focus

Let Saturday be a day to focus on what we do and why we do it. In particular we can look at our work, paid or unpaid, and the way we spend time outside work. What is our time for? Where does our effort go? What do we give, and what do we receive? What or who takes priority? The sabbath reminds us to give time to our families. How much energy and care do we put into our relationships? What religious (or other) rituals do we persist with although they have lost meaning to us? What could we begin to do to refresh our sense of spiritual devotion? On Friday night or Saturday morning, light two candles. With the first, consider how you observe God's law of love, and what you understand by it. How much is it related to your involvement with others, with all life? With the second, consider how you feel God interacts with the world and with you. Call to mind the remembrance Jesus asked of his followers, to break bread together and think of him. You might like to share a bread-breaking with friends and/or family (see Eucharist liturgy).

Canticle for Saturdays

Shalom, shalom, shalom,
My peace I give to you;
Shalom, shalom, shalom, shalom,
My peace I give to you.

(From the Eucharist liturgy)

Prayer

Blessed are You, our God, Sovereign of the Universe,
for you have willingly and lovingly given us
your holy and eternal rest for an inheritance.
Amen

(After the Hebrew household sabbath liturgy)

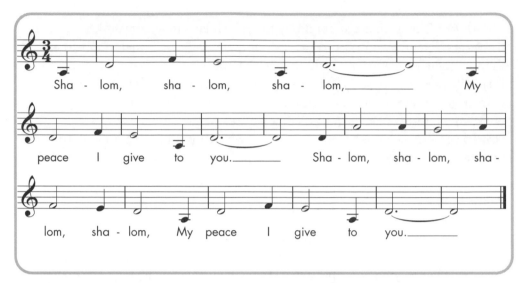

Sha - lom, sha - lom, sha - lom,_____ My

peace I give to you._____ Sha - lom, sha - lom, sha -

lom, sha - lom, My peace I give to you._____

Dawn

Let us know, let us press on to know the Lord,
His appearing is as sure as the dawn.

Hosea 6:3 NRSV

Comment on the quotation

Dawn is a time for reaffirming trust in God, whose coming is certain and whose presence will carry us through the day to come. The statement of confidence quoted above belongs to a longer passage where Hosea attributes all experiences, whether positive or negative, to God. He says that it is the Lord, Yahweh, who has torn, and he will also heal; it is Yahweh who has struck down and he will also bind up the people's wounds. The injuries referred to are troubles experienced by the people of Israel, and Hosea ascribes these troubles to the nation's infidelity towards the covenant. This quotation prompts us to look at our own understanding of whom or what God is, and the way in which we think God is involved in our lives. My response to the frequent question, 'Do you believe in God?' tends to be, 'What do you mean by God?' Even people who say they do not believe in God need to have some idea of what they don't believe in! Sometimes we find we are in agreement with others, sometimes our ideas are poles apart, but at the heart of Christian belief is an understanding shared with Hosea, that if we seek then we will find God eventually, as surely as the dawn follows night. It may be that non-believers look upon God too, but give no name to their experience.

Relevance

Dawn or sunrise is a universal symbol of hope, newness, relief, gladness, optimism. In my teenage days I was very drawn to the idea of dawn, and when on holiday I would get up early and go to watch it from whatever natural or ancient feature I had found in the area, whether it be the sea, a dolmen, a woodland or the top of a hill. I often found however that, whereas I had been hoping for spectacular beauty, as often as not dawn was a gradual diminishing of darkness into grey and then paler grey; and, as clouds were covering the sun, it would remain cold and quite damp and dull for a long while. Similarly, we might well hope that the appearance of God will be an awesome, breathtaking event. But perhaps it is not so much the theatre associated with Divine presence that is important, but the fact that dawn can be relied upon to happen: I never went out to witness the rising of the sun only to find that it did not appear at all! The fact is that the sun is already there. It is not suddenly with us; it is we on earth who gradually turn towards it. Our feelings of gladness are associated with the realisation that God has been there all the time, throughout our experience of night.

Links
Matthew 28:1, Luke 24:1 It is at early dawn, while it is not yet light, that the women go to the tomb of Jesus, hoping to anoint his body. Their sense of urgency is heightened by the early hour, and their discovery of the resurrection coincides with the first light of the day.
Mark 1:35 Jesus chose the early morning, before light, to pray in a deserted place.
2 Peter 1:19 What does the writer mean by the dawn and the day star?
1 John 1:5 God is light.
1 John 4:8 God is love.

Points of focus
Dawn, or at least the time to get up, is the first of three times during the day which Daniel devoted to prayer, an act of devotion which was noticed and used against him. For us too it is the time to open ourselves to God and rededicate ourselves in trust and obedience. To begin and end the day in prayer is to wrap the day in sanctity – all events and encounters within that time are then encompassed in God's care. You might even like to try a little bowing down, in the style of Daniel, with the kinetic prayer at the end of chapter 6. You could also turn to the east and salute the sun in some way, not as an object of worship, but as a symbol of God's constant presence: dawn is not the arrival of God, but the turning of the earth to be in God's light.

Prayer
God of the ages,
pierce the darkness of my night
with the brilliance of your presence,
bring a new dawn to my awakening soul,
that I may praise your glorious name
and reflect your light as the moon reflects the sun.
Amen

Midday

… when at midday along the road, your Excellency, I saw a light from heaven, brighter than the sun, shining around me and my companions. When we had all fallen to the ground, I heard a voice saying to me in the Hebrew language, 'Saul, Saul, why are you persecuting me?'

Acts 26:13 NRSV

Comment on the quotation

This quotation is part of the account Paul gives to King Agrippa concerning allegations raised against Paul's evangelical work. Paul refers to his experience on the road to Damascus, described earlier in Acts. Although travelling in the heat of midday, Paul describes a light even greater than the sun, associated with the Divine presence. God is connected with light elsewhere in the Bible – for example, Psalm 43 refers to God's light and truth. Holy people touched by God are also described as shining: for example, Moses coming down from Mount Sinai, and Jesus at the transfiguration. The point here, however, is not simply that Paul, formerly Saul, experienced God's light, but that the light appeared to surprise and shock him into a complete change of policy. This man who had set out in the morning to persecute Christians had virtually become one of them by lunchtime.

Relevance

The midday sun can remind us of Paul's unique experience of God's light, calling him away from everything his upbringing had taught him to be true, and compelling him to make a complete and instant U-turn in his beliefs. It reminds us that we, like Paul, have our own ideas about what is right and wrong, our own standards, our own targets for criticism. Many of these ideas have been with us since childhood, impressed on us by our parents and teachers and our life experiences. Yet, shockingly, they are not always correct. This realisation can make us feel quite insecure, perhaps reflecting the helpless blindness that came upon Paul. Losing our old beliefs is not necessarily a negative experience. It leaves a void that has to be filled, and in that moment of emptiness we become vulnerable. But it is our vulnerability that opens us to God and the message of Jesus; suddenly we are receptive and need help. To Paul, God sent Ananias who healed him. In our own moments of true disillusionment, too, God sends his messengers to leap in and fill the emptiness with new insight. We just have to be humble enough and open enough to accept them.

Links

Malachi 3:6 'For I the Lord do not change.' The people are called to change back and return to faithfulness.

The Book of Jonah: Here we read of a whole city of people who were asked to change and did, much to the chagrin of Jonah.

Matthew 3:8 'Bear fruit worthy of repentance!' Matthew records the message of John as a call to change, to make a clean start. His message is repeated by Jesus: Matthew 4:17 (and elsewhere).

Isaiah 58:6 This passage describes the true work of God: not empty piety and words, but compassionate action.

Points of focus

Midday is a time to pause, if only for a few moments, and notice what we are doing, and why. It is a time to check alignment, to remember priorities, to think about where we are going, literally or metaphorically, to recall the prayer which began the day and the prayer that will close it, and to reflect on the Shekinah, presence of God. God is there, ready to interrupt life, whether we are mindful of God or not. This, or later in the afternoon perhaps, is the second time Daniel bowed down to God in prayer. It is another opportunity for a prayer ritual, but sometimes we cannot manage this in the busy schedules by which we are driven, in which case it is enough to reconnect through Ruah, breath of God. Breathe deeply, and know that God is around you and within you.

Prayer

God of light,
sear through the cataracts of my misunderstanding
and reveal yourself,
that I may know for sure
the truth of your love,
and the reality of your power,
and be emboldened to do your will,
your will lived out
in the humanity, the selflessness,
the defiant, courageous, subversive love of Christ.
Amen

Evening

They heard the sound of the Lord God walking in the garden at the time of the evening breeze …

Genesis 3:8 NRSV

Comment on the quotation

The quotation follows the mythical account of Adam and Eve's experience of temptation in the garden of Eden. According to Genesis 2:10–14, Eden was located in Mesopotamia, origin of some of the first known civilisations and ancestral home of Abraham. The Euphrates and the Tigris, the only rivers now identifiable, have their source in Eastern Turkey near the Iranian border and mount Ararat, and both flow through Iraq. Yahweh in the story is depicted as walking in the garden, a very anthropocentric idea, but one that places the God of the Old Testament firmly on earth, enjoying its delights. God comes to the garden to meet Adam and Eve, so that they can walk with him. But he finds that they are hiding; the rift between God and humanity has begun. In the myth, Yahweh punishes the couple, but surely their punishment is the natural consequence of choosing to separate themselves. Hiding from God is the cause of pain and suffering. Walking with God in the cool of the evening is heaven on earth.

Relevance

The evening in a warm climate is very welcome, and often very beautiful. One can well imagine the writer of the Eden story seeing it as the perfect time of day in which to relax and commune both with God and with nature, in a spirit of peace and mutual trust. A Hebrew term for the presence of God is Shekinah, expressed in the feminine. We might thus associate this concept with the evening, allowing the sunset to remind us of our intended state, as creatures in fellowship with the Great Spirit, lover and origin of life. Yet there is a twinge of sadness, captured so long ago in this ancient myth but still poignant today, for the garden of Eden does not exist for us – we have left it behind and instead of walking with God we have hidden ourselves away. By this separation, we suffer. Evening time, then, is a time to contemplate right relationship with God and the earth. It is time to drop our fig leaves and reclaim our intended place in the world, because only then will we understand the world and love it enough to want to heal it and thus our relationship both with the garden and with God.

Links

Exodus 33:12–23, especially 14 The Lord promises his presence to Moses: 'I will make all my goodness pass before you.'

1 Samuel 2:21 We read here that the boy Samuel dedicated to service in the Temple, grew in the presence of God.

1 Chronicles 16:11 A song of thanks, ascribed to King David, exhorts us to seek God's presence continually.

Psalm 16:11 A song of trust and security in God: 'You show me the path of life, in your presence there is fullness of joy …'

Psalm 139:7 reminds us that the presence of God is everywhere.

John 17:5 Jesus states that he was in the presence of God before the world existed. This casts him in the role of Wisdom (Proverbs) and Logos (Gospel of John).

Points of focus

If you didn't have time at lunchtime, now is your second chance of the day to bow low in the manner of Daniel (see the end of chapter 6) and restore your focus on God. This is a time for quiet reflection and calm, time to take a few minutes out and connect with the Shekinah, presence of God, who dwells with us and wishes to walk with us in peace. It is time to notice natural beauty around us, to value the world God made, and to shed the things that we hide behind – our shame and guilt which make us believe we should not dare to approach God. We must approach God. God waits for us: *'Arise, my love, my fair one, and come away …'* (Song of Songs 2:10).

Prayer

Mother of life,
Spirit of life,
I seek healing of my relationship with you.
I seek healing of my relationship with the earth.
I seek peace of mind
that I may walk with you and know you,
and, in knowing you, come to walk with all peoples in love.
Amen

Night

I bless the Lord who gives me counsel;
in the night also my heart instructs me.
I keep the Lord always before me;
because he is at my right hand, I shall not be moved.

Psalm 16:7–8 NRSV

Comment on the quotation

We read that the night is a time when criminals prowl (Job 24:14), when the sick lie in torment (Job 7:3–4), when spirits of the dead are raised in secrecy (1 Sam 28:8) and when the full weight of grief, of loneliness, of remorse and fear are felt most acutely (Lamentations 1:2). The sense of dread is echoed in the third collect of the Evening Prayer, in the Book of Common Prayer: '*… by thy great mercy defend us from all perils and dangers of this night …*' Yet there are also many passages reminding us that the night, like the day, is governed by God, who encompasses both: '*Yours is the day, yours also the night.*' (Psalm 74:16) To the one who meditates ceaselessly on God's word and God's presence, there need be no fear, for our own perception of darkness does not mean that God is absent.

Relevance

The Bible gives us many stories of people who dream in the night, and wake knowing God spoke to them, and the quotation above surely refers to this. God gives counsel in the night; the worshipper's heart gives instruction, even in sleep. As we enter sleep, we are not alone, for God is within and around us, as close as the air we breathe, waiting for the turbulence of our minds to be stilled enough for us to hear. Not all our dreams are divinely inspired – we should not confuse the natural processes of the subconscious with God – but all the same we can be open to the possibility of communication from God. If we think about our dreams and explore their meaning, there is often some insight to be gained. Sleep is, after all, the one time we let go of our busy, rational, egotistical minds, and let something more unpredictable take over! There is a Hebrew word, *lachlom*, to dream, which is worth meditating on in the context of the biblical characters who were so moved by visions in the night. Here is an opportunity to deepen our self-understanding. The dream state unites us with the people of long ago, for whom the world of vision, dream and insight was something to be taken seriously.

Links

Psalm 23:4 Whether it is night time, or the dark valley of our own trouble, we can be reassured that God, the great shepherd, is there to guide and comfort us. Think of your own darkest nights. What brought you through them? Or do you feel that you are still walking in darkness? Pray for help, for guidance, for companionship.

Luke 6:12 We read that Jesus prayed all night before he chose his disciples. How much effort do you put into prayer when you need to make a decision?

John 3:2 Nicodemus came to Jesus by night – that is, secretly. In the book of Acts too there is much secretive night-time activity. Jesus's followers lived in dangerous times, when following the Way took great courage.

Points of focus

Jesus spent nights in prayer on the hillsides. It was in the darkness that he drew close to the light. It was at night that Nicodemus came to him, secretly seeking answers to difficult questions, embarrassed but asking nevertheless. Yet it was at night too that Jesus sweated the blood of one facing death, and it was at night that he was brought to trial before a kind of kangaroo court of religious leaders, fearful for their relationship with the Roman occupiers. The night is rich with the story of Jesus, who never bowed to the darkness of fear, but shone with courage and integrity. As you prepare for sleep, meditate on the quotation above and the idea that your heart continues to instruct you. Hand over your concerns to God in prayer, asking that you might be free of them through the night and wake with solutions clear in your mind the next morning. This is the third time to get down on your knees in prayer with Daniel!

Prayer

If today I lost myself along the way,
forgive me, Love,
and guide my wayward steps, I pray.
For I am but a child, all alone.
Come out to meet me then,
and bring me home.
Amen

Chapter 6

THE SWALLOW & THE SPARROW

~ This is my body

About this chapter

This is a book about everyday life, and the thing that goes with us all the way through that life is the body. In the process it changes a lot, but it is ours, a shell for the spirit, a home for God maybe, but a physical presence which belongs organically to the earth: from the atoms of the universe it was formed, and to the same universe it will return when we have no more need of it. Christianity has a history of being rather hard on the body. There has been plenty of mortification, and a great emphasis on separating the spiritual, which is considered of value, from the physical, of less value. There is a feeling that only those who practise asceticism, denying the physical, can enter into a spiritual life. Well, this is one dimension to faith that can be drawn out of the scriptures, but is it the way of Jesus? Jesus talks about self-discipline, about having control and exercising choice over our bodies, not allowing temptation or weakness to override our sense of God's will, and he demonstrated that for us. But Jesus was a physical person. This is a man who was criticised for enjoying his food and drink too much, who accepted the sensuality of women massaging his feet with priceless perfume and wiping them with their own hair. This is the man who broke taboo to touch lepers and corpses, who lay quite openly with his beloved disciple nestled against his chest at the last supper and took children in his arms to bless them. This is a man who loved with his body as well as his soul, and his physicality was part of his presence on earth. Our bodies are the means by which we communicate with other people; they are our own enacting of Christ's love. So there is a need for self-control and integrity, yes, but extreme mortification is not the path we are all called to follow in our ordinary lives.

This chapter looks at our bodies. We give them a lot of attention, and the time spent on them can become an opportunity for contemplation and reflection to centre us in the present moment. We can also explore the spiritual practices of other faiths, and in so doing discover new freedoms within our own. Particularly, we can think about expressing our spirituality through movement. Inspiration for the kinetic meditation at the end of the chapter came from several sources: the way in which Muslim believers move in prayer; ancient Chinese wisdom concerning body-energy; the Native American concept of the tipi which I mentioned in chapter 2 and the significance of the four directions; and Hindu yoga practices concerning the sacred breath.

The story

In the Bible, sparrows are coupled with swallows, for example in Psalm 84:3 *Even the sparrow finds a home, and the swallow a nest for herself, where she may make a nest for her young, at your altars, O Lord of Hosts …'*. Jesus mentions sparrows on their own to draw attention to the humblest, smallest and most common of God's creatures, meaning perhaps those who saw themselves or were seen by society as unimportant and unremarkable. The Venerable Bede, an 8th-century monk and English historian, tells a story about a sparrow, although it could just as easily be about a swallow, because both nest in human dwellings and given the chance fly in and out. You can find the story in its original form in Bede's *The Ecclesiastical History of the English Nation,* chapter 13.

King Edwin is in council with his elders, discussing the possibility of converting the people's faith to Christianity following his own personal conversion. The elders are receptive to the new religion, and one describes how serving the pagan gods has done nothing for him. Another gives an analogy: the king sits in company in the great hall on a stormy winter evening, feasting, discussing business and telling stories around a good fire while snow falls outside and gales howl. A sparrow comes in through a hole in the woodwork, and flies across the hall and out of a window, into the bleak sky. For the few seconds that the sparrow is inside it is sheltered from the violent weather, but soon enough vanishes back into the darkness. So it is with the life of humans, says the elder. Our lives on earth are like the flight of the sparrow through the hall. What comes before and what lies beyond is unknown, and full of mystery and dread. But Christianity offers hope and insight into this unknown, and therefore it is a teaching to be respected and followed.

Comment

We know nothing about the future, and the past is gone. We can only live in the present. Even so, it is amazing how much of the present moment we lose by worrying about both past and future, and our own place in the big picture. Jesus said *don't* worry. Matthew 6:25–26:

> *'Therefore I tell you, do not worry about your life, what you will eat or what you will drink, or about your body, what you will wear. Is not life more than food, and the body more than clothing? Look at the birds of the air; they neither sow nor reap nor gather into barns, and yet your heavenly Father feeds them. Are you not of more value than they?'*

and Matthew 10:29–31

'Are not two sparrows sold for a penny? Yet not one of them will fall to the ground apart from your Father. And even the hairs of your head are counted. So do not be afraid; you are of more value than many sparrows.'

Jesus was a master of living in the present. But he also had a firm grip on his place: where he had come from and where he was going. He had come from God, lived in and with God, and was going back to God. God is the all-encompassing reality, the great I AM, the reason why we can feel safe and secure. God knows and holds our past, our present and our future; we are safe. That frees us to live in the here and now, to be aware of the immediate, to walk in the Spirit, to value spontaneity and to give room to loving, because that is our work.

Soul friend

John the Baptist made God his security. He distanced himself from his own background as the son of a well-to-do priest, and took on simplicity, humility and courageous, justice-driven honesty. He belonged to God in the wilderness. God was his past, his present and his future. In a chapter on awareness of our own bodies, our physicality, John is helpful, as he went to extremes: his prophet-style clothes, his asceticism, his choice of living in a cave or a rough shelter in the wilderness, eating the simplest of foods, asks us to look at why we do things. Why do we wear what we wear? Why do we eat what we eat? Why do we live where we live? Why are these things important to us? What message are we giving the world by the way we present ourselves, and the way we deal with our own physicality? John, then, is a good soul friend, if a challenging one, for this chapter.

Contemplations on the body

The following provide focus for contemplation, with particular emphasis on centring thoughts on the here and now, the present moment. To do so is to remove the power of fear about the future and anxiety concerning the past; one may never happen and the other is gone. It is too easy to lose our peace of mind in worries and fantasies. Instead we can use our moments of hair-brushing and kneeling to weed the garden, bathing and foot-washing as snapshots in time, precious windows to peace.

Head

And Moses quickly bowed his head towards the earth, and worshipped. He said, 'If now I have found favour in your sight, O Lord, I pray, let the Lord go with us.'

Exodus 34:8–9 NRSV

Comment

Moses bowed down at the summit of Mount Sinai, having experienced the presence of God. God declared his name, Yahweh, meaning I AM: 'I AM, I AM, a God merciful and gracious, slow to anger, and abounding in steadfast love and faithfulness, keeping steadfast love for the thousandth generation, forgiving iniquity and transgression and sin ...' To this God, Moses bows his head, declaring his own role in the relationship. The steadfast love of which God speaks is *Hesed*, described earlier in the contemplation on friendship; it was a deeply binding, loyal and self-sacrificial expression of love. This declaration has endured the ages, and is as relevant to the Christian faith as it is to Judaism. This is our God.

Scripture links

Note that in the culture of biblical times the head was not seen as the source of the intellect – what we would call 'mind' – but of life: it is the vessel which the Ruah, the holy breath of life, enters and from which it leaves.

Matthew 8:20 The son of Man has nowhere to rest his head.

Matthew 10.30 Even the hairs of your head are numbered: how valuable you are!

Matthew 26:7 A woman anoints Jesus's head. Messiah or Christ means the anointed one. Anointing with oil was a sign of dedication to the service of God.

John 19:2 The soldiers put a crown of thorns on Jesus's head.

Colossians 1:18 Christ is the head of the body church.

Connections

- When are women and men expected to cover their heads (or not) for different reasons in different cultures? Exploring the traditions behind these customs draws us deeper into understanding our own and other cultures.

- In the Bible, as in our culture, people talked about leaders as heads. We take this to mean the person who controls from the top of a hierarchical structure. If we use the biblical understanding, however, that the head is the source of life, then we might see our heads in a slightly different light. Alternatively, it might allow us to redefine who the head actually is. Who is the life and soul of the place? Who is indispensable, so that if you took them away something of the structure would die? Consider leaders known to you personally and in terms of politics and so on. What does that person seem to understand by the concept of leadership? In what sense are they a 'head'? If you ever take leadership responsibilities, how do you communicate headship?

- Having a place to rest your head means more than having a pillow. It is about belonging and security. Jesus embraced homelessness. In what ways do we embrace the homeless, in his name?

Reflective activities

- Calm your breathing, close your eyes and imagine your head as a vessel into which Ruah flows, the holy breath of life, uniting all life. It is the Holy Spirit which Jesus breathed upon his followers. She flows in with your in-breath, in and around your body, energising you, and out into the world as you breathe out. In the present moment in which you find yourself, you are enveloped and filled by God, and so are the people with whom you find yourself; *all* the people, all life. Let this change the way you see. As you go through the day, at any time and in any place you can draw yourself back to awareness of God's presence by focusing on the breath. Use the words of Paul in Acts 17:28: *'In him we live and move and have our being.'* God is closer than the air we breathe.

Prayer

Jesus our Head,
life and soul of our fellowship,
without you our service is empty,
our words dull,
our hope dead.
To you we owe all respect, O King …

O homeless, dishevelled, foot-sore traveller king,
smelling of sweat, hair lank and clothes thick with dust,
feet blistered and thick-skinned from tramping the miles,
stomach empty, throat dry, eyes dazzled by the sun,
back aching from sleeping rough on unyielding ground,
you don't look like a great leader,
striding the hills and valleys to be with us
and spread the urgent news of God's love.
Yet you are the life and soul of our worship,
our reason why,
our inspiration and our truth.
Traveller king,
when we go into our fine buildings
to worship you with silver cups and silk garments,
exquisite choirs and sumptuously crafted stone and wood,
somehow I think I know where you are.
You are just outside lying on a bench in the sun
resting your thorn-torn head for a while,
until we will come out and spare you some change for a coffee.
Amen

Contemplations on the body: Eyes

Do not judge, so that you will not be judged … Why do you see the speck in your neighbour's eye, but do not notice the log in your own eye? Or how can you say to your neighbour, 'Let me take the speck out of your eye,' while the log is in your own eye? You hypocrite …

Matthew 7:1,3–5 NRSV

Comment

The eye is perhaps the most obvious of our sense organs. We each see from a different perspective – something we easily forget – and we each interpret the signals we receive differently. One person will notice a spider and back off in a cold sweat, while another will pick it up and gently put it outside. We see, but how we react depends on who we are and what are our previous experiences. Jesus drew attention to people's perceptions of wrongdoing: having noticed imperfection, the temptation is to criticise; we see and judge. To see, however, as he pointed out elsewhere, we need light, and most of all we need the light to shine on us and within us, so that we can see the truth about ourselves. We need to look within and perceive our own imperfections, and interpret them. Having seen ourselves in the light of truth, we know about the log in our own eye, and we learn humility. In humility, we can look outwards again, and see opportunity not to criticise but to heal – or at least to offer empathy.

Scripture links

Genesis 3:5 The serpent tells Eve that the consequence of eating the forbidden fruit will be that her eyes will be opened and she will know the difference between good and evil, like God.

Psalm 121:1 I lift up my eyes to the hills; from where will my help come?

Matthew 6:22 The eye is the lamp of the body.

Acts 9:8 Paul is blinded by the vision of Jesus, and becomes dependent on the healing touch of Ananias. What might his blindness represent? Does it give him an opportunity to look within?

Luke 19:42 Jesus weeps over Jerusalem: 'If you, even you, had only recognised on this day the things which make for peace! But now they are hidden from your eyes.' He goes on to predict the downfall of the city.

Connections

- What are the things which make for peace? Are they also hidden from our eyes? Does Jesus weep over our cities too and mourn for us?
- When you turn your eye inward and look at yourself, what do you see? Do you

judge yourself harshly? Are you willing to forgive yourself? Do you see nothing to criticise?

- When have you sought help, and found it?
- What judgements do you make about other people? Are these criticisms also true of yourself?
- What do your own eyes communicate to the world? Warmth? Humour? Sadness? Lack of interest? Disengagement? Longing?

Reflective activities
- Sit in front of a mirror and gaze like a lover into your own eyes for a long time. Your eyes are beautiful. They are unique. So are you. Love yourself, know yourself.
- Those things which make for peace, what are they? Look at the world, look at yourself, your own heart, the life of Jesus. Recognise the way of peace in the here and now. In each situation in which you find yourself, in each moment, what is the path of Shalom?
- Notice what value judgements you attach to what you see. What can you do to turn negatives into positives?

Prayer
Brother Jesus,
what disturbs the heart more
than the sight of a grown man crying?
How deep is your grief, how open your heart,
how rare are you, most precious, gentle one,
in this hard-hearted world,
to dare to weep.
I wish to comfort you;
here is my shoulder …
but I am too small to take your burden.
I try to find words but suddenly I know none.
I reach out,
but I dare not touch you, holy one;
who am I to you?
Alone you stand, your grief ocean deep,
and I stand separate at your shore, inadequate, in awe.
'Why are you weeping?' I ask,
as though I didn't know.

Dear Brother, what will stop your tears?

> *Will you smile for me,*
> *if I learn your ways of gentleness?*
> *Will you laugh with me,*
> *if I walk your path of peace?*
> *And will you take my hand*
> *and give me your love,*
> *that precious love that*
> *makes you weep*
> *for the sake of another?*
> *Amen*

Contemplations on the body: Ears

And when you turn to the right or when you turn to the left, your ears shall hear a word behind you, saying, 'This is the way; walk in it.'

Isaiah 30:21 NRSV

Comment

This quotation is taken from a passage about peace and the restoration of Zion inserted between prophecies of trouble. It is perhaps a text that was added in the light of the people's return to the land after exile, a kind of *'There, you see, God never abandoned us, we didn't really think he would ...'* statement. But the idea is of a person walking uncertainly, erring to either side, yet somehow corrected by a guiding voice directing them to leave behind an obsession with false gods and to walk 'the Way'. In those days, false gods were plentiful, but it was easy to tell what they were and thus avoid them: they were anything material, set up or made by hand and then worshipped as a source of spiritual power. Today, we can appreciate that images have a symbolic value, and that they communicate insight into the nature of God, without worshipping them. Our own idols are worse in a way. They are not even made with a spiritual function: fast cars, glamorous celebrities, money ... these and more are the things that cause us to veer off the path. But what is the voice behind us, keeping us straight? Jesus said he was the way, the truth and the light, and as he said so often to the people he taught, 'Let anyone who has ears listen!'

Scripture links

Mark 4:9 and elsewhere: Jesus, it seems, was fond of this rather cryptic phrase, which is translated in various ways. The NRSV offers, 'Let anyone with ears to hear, listen!' He used it at the end of parables, inviting people to read between the lines of his stories. But we should not consider Jesus only in the light of his stories. What are we to make of his life? He said that we should love one another. But it was what he did that demonstrated what he really meant by that: he sought out the marginalised of society, to make them feel valued, so that they could be whole and enter into life. He also challenged the leaders who were responsible for marginalising these people, to the point where they hated him. At that time, the marginalised were women, foreigners, cripples, demoniacs, lepers … Who is it now? What has happened to the real message that Jesus was teaching – the message that was so subversive that he covered his tracks with enigmatic parables?

Connections

- Do we, collectively, hear the word of Jesus as he meant it? What do you think his message was? What are the implications of that message for the way we live our lives? Is the church proclaiming Jesus's message, or a different one?
- How do you decide what is the right way to go, minute by minute?
- Jesus announced to the rejects of society that they were welcome in God's kingdom. Is that what Christians do now? Who are the marginalised closest to you at the moment? Jesus is there for them, accepting and affirming them. What opportunity do you have to do the same?
- What can you say to or do for a person that allows them to move from a feeling of marginalisation to a sense of inclusion and belonging?
- Do you feel or have you ever felt marginalised? How do you interpret the words and teachings of Jesus relative to your situation?

Reflective activities

- In conversation, when can you make clear your loyalty to Jesus's love for outsiders? Whom can you support with your voice? Whom can you support in practical ways?
- Look at your own body language. Do you send out signals of warmth and affirmation to people you see as 'different'? Are your words positive while your body recoils?
- How are your listening skills? Do you have ears that hear the stories of others with compassion and a desire for their healing? If not, how might you develop your ministry of listening?
- How easy do you find it to go against convention, to shock, to challenge, by your actions, your dress, your beliefs … ? Do it and see how it feels! What is it like to surprise people who have fixed ideas about you? What is it like to shock people you love but disagree with? Can you do it? Should you do it? How bound are you by concerns about fitting in and what people will think of you?

Prayer

Jesus, when you said 'Come out with me,'
I didn't know you were heading for the gay bar,
then the brothel,
then the asylum seekers' hostel,
then the back alleys where the druggies are getting their fixes,
then the home for delinquent children,
then the gaol …
What kind of a guy are you?
I'm waiting to talk to you, about me.
It's important;
I want to check out where I stand with you,
see if I heard you right.
But you seem to be avoiding me.
People, always people, and you're giving them all
more attention than you ever gave me.
And where are your nice friends?
So I'm standing out here, out on the street waiting for you
finally to come out of that homeless shelter,
have a shower maybe,
and then I'm going to ask once more for some quiet time, just you and me.
What are you doing in there, anyway?

What do you mean you are waiting for me to come in too?
And don't call me that.

Amen

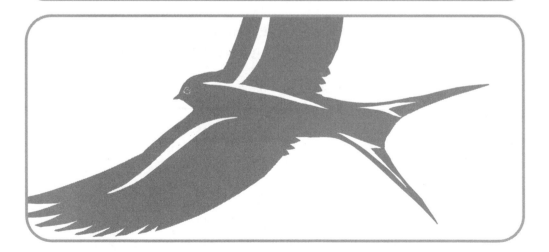

Contemplations on the body: Mouth

Then the Lord God formed man from the dust of the ground, and breathed into his nostrils the breath of life; and the man became a living being.

Genesis 2:7

Let everything that breathes praise the Lord!

Psalm 150:6

Comment

In the first of these quotations, it is Adam, the first man, that is made. This is not a reference to man- and womankind. The quotation is from the second of the creation myths offered to us in Genesis, which begins with the formation of a lone male, rather than the progressive creation of the universe that culminates in the appearance of humanity. There are connections between the two accounts, though. In particular, in the first we read of the breath or the wind of God, Ruah, which hovers over the primordial deep; in the second account, we find this same breath of God animating the man. He only has life when he is filled with Ruah, the holy, energising (feminine) breath. This same breath gives life to all. In the second quotation, from Psalm 150, 'everything that breathes' means all living things. They are living because they are energised by God's sacred breath, as was Adam. All life is united by the sharing of the breath. We all share God. In God we live and move and have our being.

Scripture links

Matthew 12:34 Out of the abundance of the heart, the mouth speaks …

Matthew 15:11–20 It is what we say that defiles us, not eating with unwashed hands!

Luke 21:15 Jesus says he will give his disciples a mouth and wisdom that nobody can contradict.

Exodus 23:13 The Hebrews are told not even to mention the names of other gods. This seems a bit extreme, but in many cultures words have great power, and to speak the name of a god or a spirit is considered on a par with summoning that being or invoking its presence. It's somewhat analogous to our use of telephone numbers: when we dial a number it puts us in contact with someone, and we have to be a little cautious about whom we contact and to whom we give our details. For telephone number read name, for dial read speak. Who are the false gods we might inadvertently be contacting?

Psalm 40:3 He put a new song in my mouth, a song of praise to God …

Connections

- With the idea that our words reflect what is in our hearts, listen to yourself speaking. What are you really saying about yourself?
- How often do you sing? The phenomenon of singing unites all cultures and peoples through history. Whether through work songs, ballads, sagas, laments or thanksgiving, emotions which are difficult to articulate in ordinary speech somehow take on a new dignity when sung.
- What false gods do you give power to by your words?
- There are plenty of musical instruments which rely on breath. What types of music do you enjoy listening to or playing?

Reflective activities

- When we breathe in, we can imagine breathing in the Ruah, the holy breath of God which unites all life. We need to take deep, confident breaths, not shallow ones, if we want to be wholly filled with God.
- What we breathe out perhaps takes a little more care. Our out-breath can carry speech. Speech can be good and it can be harmful. We are warned often in the scriptures to think before we speak: rash words are like sword thrusts, but the tongue of the wise brings healing … (Proverbs 12:18)
- Consider taking up a musical instrument, especially a wind instrument, if you don't already play one. Tin whistles, ocarinas, harmonicas and recorders are easy and satisfying to learn – and your vocal cords are a wind instrument too. Or listen to others playing: a musician in tune with an instrument communicates something of his or her soul … What feelings would you like to express through music rather than speech?
- Notice opportunities to use your voice for the sake of others. How do you use your voice to build up, to bring down, to heal or to hurt?

Prayer

My God,
How I wish I could get the balance right!
I'd like to sound wise and I sound a fool; I'd like to sound clever
and instead I demonstrate my ignorance to all the world.
I want to articulate the depth of my feeling
and I come out with sentiment that would make anyone cringe;
I'd like to speak words of truth, razor sharp,
and I hear myself missing the point, lost in vagaries,
all my words tangential to what I know I really mean.
Then of course there are the times when I just say any old thing

to fill the silence.
I start sentences without knowing where they will end,
I talk nonsense, couched in emotive words,
but avoiding expressions like 'I love you.'
Forgive me, God, and still my tongue.
Out of my heart my words tumble.
That's what worries me, O God.
Speechlessness, silence, is a balm.
After the silence,
may you whisper to me?
May you give me voice,
to articulate the love
hidden in the abyss of my heart?
Or is this something for which I need no words at all?
Amen

Contemplations on the body: Heart

But the Lord said to Samuel, 'Do not look on his appearance or on the height of his stature, because I have rejected him; for the Lord does not see as mortals see; they look on the outward appearance, but the Lord looks on the heart.'

1 Samuel 16:7 NRSV

Comment

In Ancient Middle-Eastern culture, the heart was mainly associated with what we would call 'mind'. The brain was not really understood as an organ – in mummification practices in the region, it tended to be liquidised, removed through the nose and discarded, while other organs were carefully preserved. The head was the chamber which received and released the breath, and housed the eyes and ears. Awareness was linked to the heart, centre of the life-blood, which was sacred. Thus was God concerned with the heart, for all blood and all life belonged to God. So when we read that God looks at the heart, although our own interpretation is often that God is interested in how loving we are, the biblical meaning was frequently that God sees our thoughts and understanding. The quotation above comes from the account of Samuel's anointing of David. First, each of David's brothers stands before Samuel and is rejected as God's choice for king. David is only sent for after all the elder brothers have been considered. He is God's chosen one because of inner qualities, not outer ones.

Scripture links

Matthew 5:8 Blessed are the pure in heart …
Matthew 6:21 Where your treasure is, there will be your heart …
Matthew 12:34 Out of the abundance of the heart, the mouth speaks.
Matthew 22:37 The command from the Hebrew scriptures, to love God with all your heart, mind and soul.
John 14:27 Jesus gives us peace, and tells his followers, 'Let your hearts be untroubled.'

Connections

- What thoughts and feelings do you have that you would prefer God not to know about? Is it possible for them to remain hidden?
- The ancient Hebrews must have seen God as a very intimate presence: God's Ruah, the holy breath, was within; the blood itself was of God and was intrinsically bound up with life. God was close enough to look not upon the face but

into the heart: God was within. Where is God for you, now? What makes you aware of God's presence?

- What do you think were the qualities which God saw in David's heart?

Reflective activities

- Get a drum (or improvise) and play heart-beat rhythms. Pause in what you are doing and listen to your own heart. Remember the blood in you – the life in you – is sacred, and the same is true for all those around you, and all life.
- Still your mind, and be aware that God knows and enters into your peace.
- What qualities do you hope God sees in you? What qualities would you like to have?

Prayer

Living God,
seer of my unspoken thoughts,
watcher of my fantasies and my nightmares,
projector of vision and breather of whispered wisdom
so often missed,
your presence unsettles me;
your presence disturbs and challenges.
If you are really there,
how can I ever think again
the thoughts I know I was toying with
only minutes ago,
thoughts I would not share with my best friend …
How well you know me, O God,
how well do you know my fickle heart
and my restless mind, my attention-seeking child soul,
my hunger-driven life blood.
How well you know me, minute by minute different,
day by day changing my song and story to fit the audience,
hour by hour testing your patience,
my little forays into godlessness
trying you. Are you there? Are you really there?
Oh, you are there all right, and you are here.
So forgive me my unbelief;
forgive my shamelessness,
my impertinence, my waywardness.
I know you are there, and I welcome you.

You are like a cat curled on my knee,
not judging me but choosing to be with me,
asking that I sit still for a while,
appreciating my warmth,
quietly purring.
Amen.

Contemplations on the body: Hands

Then one of the leaders of the synagogue named Jairus came and, when he saw him, fell at his feet and begged him repeatedly, 'My little daughter is at the point of death. Come and lay your hands on her, so that she may be made well, and live.'

Mark 5:23 NRSV

Comment

In the culture of the Bible lands, hands were seen as full of power – literally, not just metaphorically. Like the arm, the hand could be lifted in violence, and also in blessing. To place a hand on the head of a sacrificial animal was to identify with that creature, as though some of one's own power now rested on it. A father's blessing on his sons was not just words: the old man's strength passed into them, more powerfully through the right hand, which is why an eldest son was son of the right hand. In Genesis 48, Joseph is annoyed with his father for blessing Joseph's two sons the wrong way round: although the boys knelt in the right positions, their grandfather crossed his hands over and gave superior power to the younger. In biblical culture, the right hand was seen as the better and more 'powerful'. In

Native American culture this association with power is seen as something to be wary of: the right hand is the hand that will lift a weapon of war, while the left hand, rather than being weak or unclean, is the hand of peace to extend in friendship. In the quotation above, we see an elder of Israel full of confidence in the power of Jesus's hands. Jesus was so full of God's dynamic energy, Ruah, that he could communicate that energy through touch. The belief was continued by the early church: the Holy Spirit could be transferred by touch, and laying-on of hands was the accepted way of administering healing.

Scripture links

Genesis 48 Jacob, or Israel, crosses his hands when blessing his grandchildren.

Acts 8:14–22 A magician called Simon sees how powerful the Holy Spirit is when transferred to the faithful through the hands of Peter and John. He asks to buy the power for himself, and is criticised.

Acts 6:6 Seven members of the early Christian community are chosen to serve, and the apostles pray, then lay their hands on them, in a ceremony to confer authority.

Psalm 7:3 The psalmist claims there is no wrong in his or her hand. What does it mean, to have wrong in your hand?

Psalm 44:20 Spreading out one's hands to a god was a common worship posture. In the light of biblical understanding of hands, what does this gesture mean? Is it done to receive Divine power or to surrender human power, or both?

Luke 23:46 Jesus on the cross cries out that he puts his spirit into God's hands.

Habbakuk 3:4 Light flashes from the palms of God's hands!

Connections

- What power do you wield with your hands? What wrong do you hold in them? What blessings do you give?
- Who suffers in your place? Have you blessed them and identified with them, or do you forget that others go without sustainable livelihoods to grow your food, or suffer exploitation by multinational companies, the arms/diamonds/drugs trades and so on, to boost our stocks and shares? There are plenty of sacrificial victims to our gods of consumerism and materialism.

Reflective activities

- Look again at your hands. What do they say about you? Soft? Gentle? Strong? Powerful? Creative? Worn? Use your own hands as objects for reflection.
- Explore the beliefs of other cultures – the Chinese use of the hands to communicate *chi*, the universal energy, in healing, for example.
- Feel the power. Sit or stand quietly with eyes closed. Place your hands in front

of your chest, palms facing each other, as though holding a grapefruit. Calm your breathing. As you breathe in, hold the breath for a moment, then as you breathe out, imagine (or feel) a surge of power emanating from the palms of your hands, creating a magnet-like resistance, which stops you bringing your hands together. It is not just your mouth which is breathing out the Ruah, but your hands too. Try this three times, then gradually move your hands a little further apart with each breath, still focusing on the power. When you can imagine that you have a large ball of energy between your hands, raise it high and offer it up to God for blessing: *'This power in my hands is the power of your love. May I use it wisely. Amen.'* Repeat this meditation frequently and you might be surprised by the results!

Prayer

Jesus our Healer,
we ask you to heal us, but do we really mean it?
Do we really know, as truth, that the holy breath of God
breathes even through the skin of your palms,
your healing, power-full palms, punctured by nails,
the power ebbing away, to the cry of 'Healer, heal thyself'?
Jesus our healer, we wonder at the healings of long ago,
in the old days when people could do that sort of thing,
when people believed in mysterious powers and had more faith …
when they used spiritual energy as though it were real.
Dance and trance and great theatre,
rhythm and song and soul-talk,
and they sought to heal the soul, never mind the body.
We look on like spectators watching sharks swimming in an aquarium.
It's powerful and scary, but it's not our world, not our way of being;
that old biblical way is alien to us,
your healings threaten our perception of how the world works.
It's mechanics we seek, to fix the nuts and bolts of our bodies, never mind the soul.
But no – I believe, so help my unbelief.
Touch me, place your hands on me,
bless me, empower me and heal me.
It is your way that I seek,
that I may give the same gift of healing to my brothers and sisters.
Amen

Contemplations on the body: Belly

Just as you do not know how the breath comes to the bones in the mother's womb, so you do not know the work of God, who makes everything.

Ecclesiastes 11:5 NRSV

Comment

The greatest of wonders is reflected here: the beginning of life. Yes, we know more about biology than people in ancient times did, but life itself is still a mystery to us. In biblical thought, life came when God breathed Ruah – the sacred, energising breath – into a being. When the breath left the body, that was death. Somehow, it seemed, God must enter into the womb to breathe into the foetus and give it life; God was there in the mother's womb, the most miraculous place in the universe. Thus, anything born of woman, or other female creature, was enlivened by the sacred breath of God which unites all life. This affirming belief challenges the doctrine of original sin, the suggestion that we are born sinful and must be baptised before our souls will be accepted in heaven. But knowing what we do about womb-time, we know that the 'breath' comes to the child through the umbilical cord, along with food. The breath and the energy needed for growth are received by the unborn into the belly. The Ruah first enters us not through the mouth, which remains closed, but within the centre of our 'inner being'.

Scripture links

Song of Solomon 7:2 (see contemplation on nourishment.) A lover delights in the beautiful navel of his beloved.
Psalm 139:13–18 The psalmist declares that God forms us in the womb.
Ezekiel 16 Ezekiel presents the image of a newborn child horribly neglected, unwashed, her umbilical cord uncut, abandoned to die. God rescues the child and helps her to grow to adulthood, yet she is faithless. This is an analogy with Israel.
Genesis 2:7 God has to breathe into Adam's nostrils, because he is formed unnaturally, as an adult.
Ephesians 3:16 'I pray that, according to the riches of his glory, he may grant that you may be strengthened in your inner being with power through his Spirit … so that you may be filled with all the fullness of God.' The inner being is that which God sees, as opposed to the outer being, which other people see.

Connections

• We pray to God to fill our bellies: give us today our daily bread. What do we do in turn to ensure that others do not go hungry?

- What can be done in this and other cultures to restore the true dignity and self-worth of women, whether they bear children or not?
- Several ancient philosophies teach that the abdominal region is the natural centre of the body's spiritual energy. How can this idea be used in Christian meditation?
- Luke 6:19 and Luke 8:46 describe power leaving Jesus, first through his hands as he touched others, but also through his body as a woman touched his clothing. What was this spiritual power? Do we have it? If not, what is laying-on of hands supposed to achieve?

Reflective activities

- In ancient Chinese art, wise sages were depicted with huge bellies, representing the immense chi or divine energy they had, and which they used for the benefit of others, for example in healing. A skinny person in art represented the spiritually undeveloped. This is why the Buddha is often portrayed with a large stomach: he has not been over-eating; he is full of sublime energy! It is worth exploring the teachings of other faiths and their meditational practices – perhaps there is wisdom which can support or inspire our own spiritual development.
- Sit (on the floor, cross-legged if possible) with your eyes closed, and imagine yourself as a Native American tipi! (See head contemplation.) At your centre is a smouldering fire. Blow on it a little and watch the flames spring up. Over the fire is a cooking pot full of water. Watch as the fire gradually heats the water, changing it from stillness to energetic bubbling. With the change, steam rises up through the tipi and out through the hole at the top. Your spirit is changed, energised, by your inner fire, a fire which feeds on the holy breath of God.

Prayer

Great Mother of All,
Breather of life-breath,
holy womb-home, nourisher, bearer of all,
flow your love into me,
pump your energy into me,
and your sacred breath,
let it surge
deep into the centre of my inner being,
like a fountain of living water,
filling me from within.

Great Mother of All,
Breather of life-breath,
I would curl in your womb-safe cradling for ever,
drinking in the warm darkness, unaware of the world beyond.
But you nourish me to send me out,
and you push me out of my sanctuary with a cry that hurts,
to love me again in a new way,
to see me grow, strangely separate from you,
to watch me learn to love and be loved,
to wait for the day when the love in me is ripe to be shared
and to bear fruit of its own,
and that day to rejoice,
Amen

Contemplations on the body: Knees

Although Daniel knew that the document had been signed, he continued to go to his house, which had windows in its upper room open towards Jerusalem, and to get down on his knees three times a day to pray to his God and praise him, just as he had done previously.

Daniel 6:10 NRSV

Comment

It was for this crime, of worshipping his God rather than King Darius, that Daniel received a sentence of death by lions. Daniel knew of the law which forbade prayer to anyone but Darius. He probably also knew it was a law written deliberately to trap him. But it made no difference to Daniel's behaviour: he followed the same prayer routine as usual, in the same place as usual. He didn't even move away from the window so that people would not see him, or limit his prayer to inactive meditation. Kneeling down was part of his prayer and he was prepared to face death rather than stop doing it. This courage we see today in countries where people are persecuted for their beliefs. Although it is safer to stay secret and make no visible sign, people continue to speak out, to act in ways which demonstrate the strength of their convictions, and like Daniel they are punished for it. Daniel, amazingly, survived his ordeal in the lion pit. But prisoners of conscience are not always so fortunate. In the face of the example they set, the least we can do is to kneel or bow down like Daniel, three times a day, and be humble.

Scripture links

Philippians 2:10 At the name of Jesus, every knee shall bow.

John 13 Jesus washes his disciples' feet, saying, 'Do you know what I have done for you?'

Psalm 95:6 A call to bow down and worship God on our knees.

Isaiah 58:5–9 The voice of God speaks through Isaiah, declaring that empty displays of humility such as fasting and bowing down in worship are without value: God's fast is that we stop injustice, free the oppressed, share food with the hungry and shelter the homeless.

Connections

- Do you ever kneel in prayer? Does your posture make any difference?
- Who makes you feel humble?
- Have you ever found yourself grovelling because you want something?
- What is the difference between servility and Christian service?
- Are there people whom you worship? How can you stop yourself?
- Are there things that you worship? For the ancients it was graven images. What are our false gods? What do you think about the resurgence of interest in nature spirits? Are they false gods, or might emanations of God's spirit exist in the natural world? (Biblically, God breathes Ruah into all life to animate it …)
- Are our rituals of worship empty, or do they come laden with the effort we have put into service of others, according to the word of Isaiah? There is no point pretending to humble ourselves in worship if we ignore the true fast which God requires.

Reflective activities

- If you are able to, commit yourself to kneel down three times a day – or at least bow your head in memory of Daniel and all prisoners of conscience – to offer prayer to God for justice, peace and freedom. This might present a challenge: we do not necessarily want to be seen praying. Apart from the fact that it might be embarrassing, Jesus did after all tell us to go quietly into a room and shut the door when we pray, so as not to attract attention. He also said, however, that we should get together with others to worship, so perhaps you might sometimes be able to gather with others at some point in the day. At the end of this chapter is a prayer routine which you might like to use.

- Consider your own true fast: your own contribution to the liberation of the oppressed, the feeding of the hungry, the sheltering of the homeless … None of us single-handed can solve all the world's problems, but we each play a small part. What is yours? Consider it not with pride, but as your true offering of worship to God. Can we stand before God offering our praises if we have done nothing?

Prayer

Brother Jesus,
I am glad you said we should lock ourselves in our rooms to pray
quietly where no one will see.
That gives me the excuse I need
not to be public about my faith,
not to be seen bringing religion into everyday life,
not to be noticed trying to connect with a spiritual reality,
in this materialistic world in which we live.
Thank you for giving me permission to be secret,
and hide my beliefs.
But then, you said not to hide our light.
And prayer gives light within,
and you yourself strode the land without fear,
delivering your message.
You said what you thought,
you rocked the boat,
you set the cat among the pigeons,
and you bowed your knee, to God,
to the ones you loved and served,
but never to the regime which killed you.
Give me courage, my brother,
to demonstrate my faith as boldly as Daniel, as boldly as you, no matter what,
and to kneel before God and my brothers and sisters in service
for the sake of justice, peace and freedom,
but never to bow down to the false gods
and corrupt powers of this world.
Amen

Contemplations on the body: Feet

I am Jesus whom you are persecuting. But get up and stand on your feet; for I have appeared to you for this purpose, to appoint you to serve and testify to the things that you have seen …

From Acts 26:15–16 NRSV

Comment

The words in Greek and Hebrew for foot are related to the concept of a firm base which will support a structure. In the dream of Nebuchadnezzar he is troubled by seeing a statue of himself which has a golden head but feet of clay that crumble under the weight, so that the statue falls: it is a sign that his dynasty will come to an end. Feet must be load-bearing. The quotation above is taken from the dramatic account of Paul's conversion. Experiencing a blinding flash, he falls to the ground, but Jesus tells him to stand up on his feet and be ready to bear witness to him. It is a command to brace himself for a challenge that will take his whole strength and commitment. Real Christian witness potentially requires the same of anybody. Christianity is not something to approach from a position of weakness. Jesus doesn't want us sprawled abject on the floor; we are no use like that. The Way of Jesus is a way of life that requires courage, strength and firm foundations, and we need to be ready for the challenges which will confront us.

Scripture links

Psalm 94:18 When I thought my foot was slipping, God held me up.

Genesis 18:4 Abraham greeted the three messengers with true hospitality, offering them water for their feet, shade from the sun and his best food.

Exodus 3:5 Moses is told to remove his sandals because he is standing on holy ground.

Psalm 40:2 God sets my feet upon a rock: a double image of strength and stability.

Isaiah 52:7 How lovely on the mountains are the feet of the messenger who brings news of peace!

Mark 1:7 John the Baptist, who was much respected as a prophet in his day, is recorded as professing his complete humility before Jesus. The feet were the lowliest part of the body, and their coverings were even lower; to remove them was the task of a slave (or woman …). Anything to do with anointing, falling at and weeping at another's feet is a clear sign of humility. Jesus, of course, performed the act of foot-washing for his disciples (John 13).

Connections

- We don't often wash one another's feet – the need is no longer there for most of us. So how do we extend hospitality? How do we express humility? What is the difference between humble service and sycophantic abasement?
- What have you seen of God's power that you can testify to? What message is it that you can convey to the people you meet, through your actions as much as your words?

Reflective activities

- Wash your own feet, massage and care for them and reflect on the spiritual need to have a strong base to stand on. Perhaps you feel moved to perform the same service for another.
- Look at the shoes you wear. Are you comfortable, so you can stand firmly on the rock God has put under your feet?
- Walk outdoors, find a good-sized rock and stand on it. Barefoot even! Say or sing to yourself, or out loud, the words of Psalm 40: 'He set my feet upon a rock, making my steps secure. He put a new song in my mouth, a song of praise to our God.'
- Practise the following: Stand straight, feet slightly apart, knees relaxed, arms by your sides, head up, back straight, shoulders relaxed … Calm your breathing, and feel the ground beneath your feet. Affirm to yourself that God's rule of love is the foundation on which you stand, and you are ready to communicate that love. You can do this anywhere, even for a few seconds, to re-ground yourself.

Prayer

Jesus my Lord and teacher,
you were the messenger who came over the mountains,
with news of peace.
How lovely on the mountains are the feet of the peace-proclaimer …
You with your disciples, tramping the land –
were your feet lovely?
Were they not dirty, broken-nailed, smelling of sweat,
dry-skin cracked, blistered from the rubbing of your simple sandals,
bramble-scratched, aching, hot and tired?
Not so lovely then.
It's easy to kneel and bathe the feet of the beautiful,
those who have time and inclination to care for themselves,
to make even their lowliest parts baby-soft and sweet-smelling.
It was not to the soft, well-manicured feet of the refined

that you knelt.
You took into your hands
rough, dirty brokenness, flesh made ugly by poverty and labour.
You accepted without judgement, you washed in tenderness,
the lowliest, most unappealing part of each disciple.
Your gentleness, your humility, your acceptance and love
give to me,
that I may learn to do the same.
Amen.

Contemplations on the body: Fingers, heart, mind and soul – bead prayer

Rejoice always, pray without ceasing, give thanks in all circumstances; for this is the will of God in Christ Jesus for you.

1 Thessalonians 5:16–18

Our fingers, like our minds, prefer to be busy. Giving the fingers something to manipulate can ease both body and mind. Paul said we should fill our minds with prayer and thanksgiving, and it makes sense to do a practice that influences both. Many world faiths use a string of beads as an aid to meditation, each bead marking the repetition of a sacred word, prayer or personal mantra. A well-suited mantra, or life song, is said to act as a positive, healing vibration through the whole body and soul, energising the one who brings it to mind if only for a moment. Evidence suggests that this ancient practice originated among people of the Hindu culture. Sikhs use a string of 108 beads to utter the sacred word *Waheguru*, Wonderful Lord. Muslims use a string of 99 beads and meditate on the glory, supreme greatness and praise due to God, or the 99 beautiful names of Allah. Tibetan Buddhists use a string called a *mala* with which they centre the mind to meditate upon a mantra or life song personal to the individual. Roman Catholics use a rosary to assist repetition of devotional prayers. Although Protestant reforms criticised the use of repetitive memorised prayer and curtailed the practice of praying with beads, their use holds us in communion with people of many other faiths through time and across the world. To pass a string of beads, one by one, through the fingers, and with each bead to repeat a word or a phrase that has deep meaning to oneself, is seen as a means to practise mindfulness of the present moment and to keep one's thoughts centred on all that is holy and immediate. Once a person has mastered the art of using prayer beads regularly, the word or prayer will gradually filter into the subconscious and remain there all the time, on the tip of the tongue and at the back of the mind, infusing the self with calm and a sense of the presence of God.

While prayers and sacred words have been prescribed through time and in different cultures, there is another approach. If using prayer beads is a method that appeals to you, the right prayer will come to you in the course of your own meditation, and will change according to need. A beginning is to make or acquire a string of beads – it might be a necklace or a bead string from another faith. You might like to decide on a number of beads, perhaps a multiple of twelve for the twelve apostles or the twelve tribes, perhaps the number of books in the Bible, or Jesus's age when he died, or your own age at the moment. Then let words come. What word or prayer might most appropriately fill your thoughts, drawing you into the present moment? Is it one of the following?

Peace
Shalom
Harmony
Agape
Maranatha
Jesus Christ
Holy Wisdom
I AM …
Wonderful Counsellor, Mighty God, Everlasting Father, Prince of Peace … (Isaiah 9:6)
In him we live and move and have our being … (Acts 17:28)
Peace I leave with you, my peace I give to you … (John 14:27)
Steadfast love and faithfulness will meet;
Righteousness and peace will kiss each other … (Psalm 85:10)
As a mother comforts her child, so I will comfort you … (Isaiah 66:13)
The Lord is my strength and my song (Psalm 118:14)

Or is it the Lord's Prayer, or a song that you know, or words from the wisdom of another tradition?

Like a dripping tap, gradually the word or words you have chosen will fill your mind to overflowing, so that this becomes the reality behind your present moment and the thought to which you return. But settle on a word or phrase with which you resonate, one that excites you or touches you deeply, because while vain repetition is an empty exercise, filling the mind with peace is not. The intention is not that the mind becomes disengaged from reality in concentrating on or remembering a word, but that the subconscious or the soul is filled with a healing vibration that will resonate through the body and bring relaxation.

Bead strings can also be really helpful in learning longer passages of scripture, each bead representing a verse or a couple of lines. Committing a scripture to memory is the age-old way of 'knowing' it. In the case of many parts of the Bible, before any words were ever written down they were passed on by word of mouth over many years by people with good memories. In cultures throughout time and across the world, the story-tellers and song-singers have always been deeply respected as guardians of the people's wisdom and tradition, having tremendous capacity to recall words reaching way back to the time of the ancestors. So go for it!

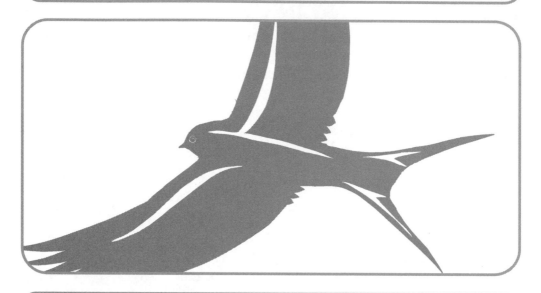

The Daniel meditation – a kinetic contemplation for the whole body

Although Daniel knew that the document had been signed, he continued to go to his house, which had windows in its upper room open toward Jerusalem, and to get down on his knees three times a day to pray to his God and praise him, just as he had done previously.
Daniel 6:10 NRSV

Physical movement while praying or meditating is accepted practice in several world faiths; yoga and tai chi are spiritual practices as much as bodily exercises; Muslims perform salah, the five prescribed times to bow down and pray. There is something of value to be learned from these traditions that can only be accessed by experimenting with kinetic prayer ourselves. Maybe it awakes a real sense of the Holy Spirit as we deepen our breathing. Maybe it relaxes us so that we can open more fully to God. Maybe the movements themselves are significant; certainly getting down on our knees and bowing our head to the ground prompts an attitude of humility. Maybe there is a symbolism of the body that we can bring to our prayer, so that each touch of the head, each raising of the hand and shifting of the feet means something to us, and with practice stirs something deep in our subconscious or, as Paul would say, our inner being.

So here is a mind-body-spirit meditation which can be used as a three-times-a-day kinetic contemplation in honour of Daniel, vegan, visionary and political subversive, great mind, dream interpreter and lover of God, who dared to ignore the king's edict and bowed down three times a day to worship the true God, not a false one. He got thrown to the lions on the strength of it, yet protected by God lived to tell the tale. The meditation as it appears here has been used in worship, but it has also grown from this form in several different ways, depending on the context in which it is to be used and who is using it. It is thus a prototype and very much offered as a stimulus for your own experiments with moving prayer, rather than a fait-accompli. The main situation in which the prayer has become relevant in worship, incidentally, is in working on Christian forms of prayer that could be used in harmony with Muslim brothers and sisters during Ramadan, the holy month of prayer and fasting.

While the meditation has some limited physical value in providing five minutes of gentle aerobic exercise, the spiritual value is obviously only accessed through thinking about the meaning of each action. For a fuller sense of the meaning, it might help to refer back to the preceding passages, or to develop your own ideas. For an abbreviated form in a confined space, or to meet special needs, stay on your feet or a chair but bow your head, or find your own way that suits you better! It is quite satisfying to repeat the sequence four times, turning to the four directions to extend your hands and offer your service to the whole earth. There is also a Native American significance in the four directions referred to in chapter 8: 'Communion with Place', which might seem appropriate to use.

WHAT TO DO

Reflection
Stand with your feet firmly on the ground.

Our foundation and strength is the word of Christ.
'Here am I, send me!' (Isaiah 6:8)

Close your eyes and breathe deeply, in and out, three times.
Ruah, Spirit of God, flows through us.

'In God I live and move and have my being.' (Acts 17:28)

Stretch your hands up above your head and lift your palms skywards.
You are like a lightning conductor, connecting heaven and earth.
'Our Father in heaven, hallowed be your name. Your kingdom come, your will be done on earth as it is in heaven.' (Matthew 6:9–10)

Bring your hands down to touch your head, and pause. 'Christ is my head.'
Fold your hands together over your heart … 'Christ is my heart.'
Then after a pause, over your belly. 'Christ is my nourishment.'
Take your hands from your belly and spread them outwards
in a gesture of blessing. 'Grace to all, and peace from God …'

Get on your knees, then bow down so your forehead touches the floor three times, a pause between each (or bow your head three times).
'I humble myself before you, O God, who is all that is good,
in sorrow for my weakness
in gratitude for your blessings
in need of your guidance and your love.
Amen'

Return to your standing position, and focus on your breathing (as above).
'In God I live and move and have my being.'

Put your hands together, as though in prayer, and bow.
'Into your hands I surrender my Spirit.'

Either repeat for the four points of the compass, so that you have extended your hands in love to all the world, or open your eyes and end the meditation.

Chapter 7

THE SWAN

~ Beloved, let us love one another because God first loved us

About this chapter

This chapter is about exploring the triangular relationship between self, God and everyone else – a relationship ultimately defined by love. The love of the soul for God and vice versa has been described vividly by mystics of many faith traditions, who seek to express in words how all-consuming that love is. The closest analogies they can find are the intensity of feeling between lovers, and the bond between parents and their children. To be separated from this love is to suffer, and none of us is a stranger to this experience. Separation causes feelings of anxiety, depression, exhaustion, disillusionment and confusion about how we can ever come to love those who hurt us, to the extent that the mystical ideal of blissful union with God may seem a far-off and unrealistic dream. But the gospel message is that the love is real, and in a way the story I have chosen illustrates that.

The idea of the mystical journey, however, usually arises from the contemplative tradition, which in turn tends to be associated with those who have devoted their lives to prayer. This is far removed from our own experience of everyday life, in which it is often hard to find space for prayer time and retreat. The way that Jesus presented to his followers brought them to the knowledge of God's love via a different route. Although Jesus himself spent long hours in prayer alone in the hills, he did not tell his disciples to do the same in order to know God's love; instead, he told them to love one another. His love for God and God's love for him led him to a life of compassionate, sacrificial giving. Throughout the pages of the New Testament we are told that we cannot pretend to love God if we do not love one another. Seeking an intimate, loving relationship with God without loving others is pointless. And we cannot fully understand what love is until we appreciate how much God loves us. The people we meet in everyday life are the inspiration for our meditation. Our own weakness and failure in loving others provides the lessons we need about the true value of God's grace.

The story:
The Dream of Angus, an ancient Irish myth

Angus was the son of the Irish Father god, the Dagdae, and the goddess Boand of the river of the same name (now the Boyne). Angus was thus superhuman. He was well known as a bit of a lad, but one night all this changed. He dreamed that the loveliest maiden in the whole of the land came to him, her feather-soft hair and pure white gown shimmering as though lit by an inner light; yet although she beckoned him to her, she was untouchable. On waking, he longed to find her, but had no idea where to look. The very thought of her took away his appetite. That night she came again, this time with a harp, her voice enchanting as she sang. Many times that year Angus had the same vision, and it affected his health. He would not eat, and lost interest in all but the thought of her. He became more and more ill, and the best healer in the land was called to his bedside. This healer, Fergne, a wise and perceptive man, knew what was wrong without being told: 'You are lovesick,' he said, and sent for Angus's mother. Boand heard the tale sympathetically and sent her messengers away for a year to search for the girl, but with no success. When the year was up, the healer Fergne sent for Angus's father. 'Why ask me?' said the god. 'He just needs to pull himself together!' But, although not convinced that this was anything but fantasy, in the end he was persuaded to help as it seemed Angus would otherwise die. Another year passed, but this time the Dagdae's envoys returned with the news that they had found her. Angus was taken to a lakeside some distance away where 150 girls were gathered, and there, without a shadow of doubt, was the woman of his dreams. But the girl, whose name was Caer, although real, remained beyond his reach. Caer's father eventually admitted that his daughter was not in his power, for she was a spiritual being: on the evening of every second Samhain, the autumnal festival, she and her companions went to the shore of a great lake, and there they became swans, she the most graceful of them all, distinguished by a thread-fine chain of gold around her neck. She and her companions would remain as swans for the year, becoming human again the following Samhain. So Angus's patience was tried for a third year, as he waited for her transformation. Finally that day drew close, and Angus went to the lake. He saw Caer, now a swan, wearing the same golden chain, and called her name. 'Who is calling me?' the swan-maiden asked. 'It is I, Angus,' he replied. She came willingly, gladly even, but insisted that he promise she would remain free, and able to return to the water. Agreeing to this condition, Angus took the form of a swan, perhaps through her magic or his own, or a bit of both, and the couple circled the lake three times, singing a song of such haunting beauty that all who heard it fell asleep for three days, giving the couple time to leave for the home of Angus's parents, and finally on to his own home, Bru na Boinne, to share their lives together.

Comment

In many ways I see the story of Angus's dream – his waiting and longing, his journeying and union – as a description of the soul's mystical experience of seeking and finding God. God is the object of all desire and all that is worth living and dying for. Like the girl who comes to Angus in a dream, it is God who comes to us and calls us to wake up from secular life and find love – but then, most helpfully to us, having found it, to return to life and get on with living, now secure in love. Often in mystical literature, such as the medieval Christian writing *The Cloud of Unknowing*, the human soul is portrayed as female, longing for her lover. It has been said that the Song of Songs in the Bible is an expression of the same: *'I will seek him whom my soul loves. I sought him, but found him not.'* (Song of Songs 3:2b) In this story, though, the soul is represented by Angus, and that which the soul seeks by the swan maiden. Having found her, he not only has the love he sought, but has also become what he sought. Transformed, he re-enters life.

Soul friends

Mary Magdalene and the beloved disciple, said to be John, are soul friends for this chapter, because according to tradition they represent the ones who hold the special relationship with Christ. As we identify with them we come to see how each soul that draws close to God is beloved. There is a name, given by God through the prophet Nathan to the baby Solomon, which means Beloved of the Lord: Jedidiah (2 Samuel 12:25); surely, to be Jedidiah is our soul's greatest desire, and ultimately, our true identity. It is a name reflected in John's gospel in the person of the beloved disciple, and perhaps in Mary too: beloved of the Lord.

Creative expression as exploration

The poems and prayers that follow explore the spirituality of relationship. There is sanctity within relationships in their own right – Christ's presence in love shared. But there in the struggling, the brokenness, the loneliness and the sense of confusion and guilt that also flavour our relationships, we can look back and trace the path of our journey to God. Sometimes it is when we struggle to love and be loved that we learn the most. Only by making mistakes do we appreciate the true value of forgiveness, the love contained in God's grace. Only when we have fallen do we understand our need for help, our gratitude to the one who comes to us and calls us out of the wilderness of our own weakness. Every experience is part of the process of discovery. Even broken relationships are not wasted time: all teach us about what love is, and what love is not, and so we grow. Our relationships speak to us of God in the course of our everyday life; they are the arena in which we work out and live out our faith. They are bound up with the heart (or the guts, if you have read chapter 6!), and it is the heart that God sees.

Trying to articulate feelings – or paint them, or play them – however clumsily, I find clarifies something in my own understanding of myself. It is a therapeutic activity, and part of the process of resolving issues. It is something not to plan for, but to allow for. I find myself doing it in spare minutes: a poem scribbled on the back of a shopping list; a collage thrown together in the hour before bed from a newspaper headline and some pictures from a magazine; a quick burst of music-making, eyes closed, playing any old thing wherever the melody takes me. One of the books I used to love looking at with my parents was called *You Are an Artist*, with pictures by children and other people from many different cultures. The title sank into my subconscious and I never doubted that I was an artist; I just got on with it. The same is true of all branches of creativity. You are a musician. You are a dancer. You are a poet. You are, and so am I. It is good to be free of the constraints that limit our free expression and tell us there is a certain way to write a poem or paint a picture. Formal education sometimes traps the soul, whereas it should give the confidence and the inspiration to fly. So it's time for some creative freedom! The following are simply explorations of relationship through poetry and prayer. Rather than take these as anything particularly special, please see them as a catalyst to inspire your own creative soul-searching on the journey of love.

The parent

The shielding place

My mother is the shielding place
where sits my soul for comfort
when the storm winds blow.
My mother is the earth-womb rocky cave,
the deep, dark water-dripping sanctuary
into which I crawl and huddle,
lost soul that I am today.
My mother is the hiding place,
the safe space
and the stillness of the night
where for a while at least
I can be comforted,
her blanket darkness holding all.

Life in her and through her
My mother is the rocking one,
the holding one,
the one whose breast
rises and falls,
rises and falls,
teasing the pebble shoreline,
her fingers white foam playing.
My mother is the rocking one,
the great, wide welcoming one,
the one whose depths
yield abundant nourishment,
and I her little one,
white-winged one,
diving one,
hungry to take and eat,
knowing nothing else
but life in her and through her.

Greeting the newborn
Child of my blood and body,
you I will give my life for,
to hold you and to nurture you
and then to let you go;
to protect you from my own weaknesses,
to hold you above my own turmoil
until you are strong enough
to deal with your own;
and to love you,
always.

On clean and unclean
I see nothing of disgust
with my own little child,
just acceptance of how he is
and a desire to meet his every need.
His birthing
does not make me unclean,

but confers supreme wholeness.
Christ our mother* undoes taboos,
She touches and allows herself to be touched.
She enters where others will not go,
she affirms what others avoid,
she sits with the dirty ones,
she declares clean
that which has been called unclean.

*The medieval mystics Julian of Norwich and Anselm explored the concept
of Christ our Mother.

Trust
The sky is afire,
my heart is afire.
He said *'Be careful'*;
I am careful,
full of care.
Light fades and dark rises
as I walk my son home,
his little hand in mine
full of trust.
Where are we going,
oh where are we going
sweet World Changer?

My father is the ocean
My father is the great singing one,
the gentle playing one,
awesome and beautiful,
fearsome and lovely;
my father is the ocean,
who is and was and always will be;
drenching me as I stand
protesting and uncertain on the shore,
waiting for the day when I will learn to surf
his tireless wild waves
and love his power for what it is.

Self and others

Fear says *fight*

This sea is too rough,
and I too weak;
my environment too huge,
and I too small.
So hard, just to keep my head above water;
when my body tires I will drown.

Fear says *fight*,
and I drain my energy, struggling,
calling to nobody;
nobody comes.
Nobody knows I am here.
Then comes exhaustion.

Exhaustion says *stop*.
I stop struggling.
I stop resisting.
I stop protesting and thrashing around.
Even my panic stops.
What does it matter?

I surrender to my drowning,
prepare myself
to embrace darkness,
to embrace pain,
to embrace the insignificance of my life.
But the water itself says *life matters*;

back to the air I rise.
The water supports me, rocks me,
calm now, whispering *trust me*,
not drowning me,
but cradling me.
Here is my God.

Living on the edge

Confident, cheerful, carefree people
surround me and hem me in,
exclude me with their shared laughter,
misunderstand my reticence for unfriendliness:
'Why didn't you come out with us?'
'Because nobody called me, nobody said *come with us*,
nobody said *see you there*,
nobody said *want a lift*?'

You don't know until you go there,
how hard it is to invite yourself in
when nobody seems to care
whether you are there or not.
You don't know how it feels
to stand on the outside of the door, wavering,
until the door closes in your face.

Jesus stands at the door and waits.
He and I got talking to each other,
together on the doorstep in the cold.
I go out with him a lot now,
because he always says, 'Come with me,'
and I need that,
it gives me confidence.

Temptations

I struggle sometimes Lord,
temptation seems so sweet and seductive, and I am weak.
I transgress, I confess, I digress once again
from my chosen path, or the path that I choose when it suits me.
I self-justify, self-analyse, self-criticise, self-hypnotise almost,
for how else could it happen,
this repetitive stumbling, this tripping and falling?
Lord you have watched many children growing.
Discerning discipline is part of love, I know.
Help me then, weakness accepted, to move on,
because I don't see an end to it, myself.
Amen

On being surprised

Usually I find you cold,
rude even and thoughtless,
so hard to touch.
Your sudden gentleness
was a flower growing up through
a sea of tarmac;
what else is there underneath
that you hide?

Where is peace?

I'm saying 'Peace, peace,'
but deep in my lungs is a raging fire of fury
that will flash out volcano-like to burn and choke.
I cry peace
but in my mind is turmoil,
the city-smashing waves of a tsunami surging inside.
I write songs of peace,
but in my heart there is grief as great as a mountain
and deep as an abyss
for the fragility, the vulnerability, the brokenness,
the trust we need in the goodness of life,
even to step out of our refuges and into the battle zone;
for where is there not a struggle for justice now?
Where is there peace?

Even the clouds look angry and the trees thrash their branches.
On the roof a gang of magpies gather, loud-mouthed.
Where is peace?
But in the gale my neighbour is singing
and hanging out her sheets on the line;
the wind is playing with her hair and teasing her skirts;
there in her back yard is peace.

Accepting the humanity of another
Disappointment pressing on my chest,
I am forced to accept the humanity of another,
the weakness I had hoped was strength,
the breaking point I had hoped
was not there at all.
But to rely on nobody is lonely,
to trust nobody is unloving.
to take risks is to open yourself again and again
to the let-down,
but also to the possibility of surprise.
Forgive me my expectations,
forgive me that I turned to anyone but you;
and, then, teach me to forgive.

Turning blame to blessing

You hurt me;
you angered me,
I blame you
for my pain;
you abused your power over me.
You are strong and I am weak.
I am the victim, you the aggressor.

But wait.
Who gave you power over me?
I claim my power back.
Who wrote the script?
I change the words.
Now, my heart is sanctuary,

my soul a hearth fire
and you will come in peace
or not at all,
your weapons left at my door.

For I the hurt one am now
a healed healer;
I the angered one
have a dove nesting in my heart.
I the frightened one
welcome you in peace,
for you are as powerless as I,
in the eternity of God.

You are simply my sister–brother,
and I yours,
for ever,
so sit here
in the light of my hearth fire
and share
my bread and wine
and share my life in this moment,
and go back to your own in love.

The lover

The kindly one
My love first came as the kindly one
who finding me snare-caught
stooped to set me loose,
and I the hare,
sore-pawed and careless,
wary even of his gentle hand,
but taking freedom all the same.

On submission and surrender
I misunderstood;
I mistook loving service for servility,
confidence crumbled into submission,
I found myself used and hurt.
I have let myself become the weak, passive,
vulnerable player in the game,
and have become,
in attempts to snatch back my power,
manipulative,
bitter and cold.
I see now,
the submission of the weak is a pitiful thing;
but how can I ever become strong enough
for my surrender to be truly beautiful to God?

A young stag is my Christ love*
My love is a young stag
melting into the forest,
silently leaping, drawing deeper
ever deeper into the dark green of life,
where hides my doe-gentle soul,
waiting to be found
in brown-eyed longing;
a young stag is my Christ love

and I his willing one,
hidden in the greenwood
of the great King.

* In the Song of Songs, the lover describes her beloved as a gazelle or a young stag

Vigil at the tomb*

My beloved sleeps the longest sleep,
his body ivory cold, his gaze veiled for ever,
his soul has slipped away upon the wind;
no more pain now beloved;
your bruised head I would cradle
but gone you are from my touch;
though I whisper my love
no more may I hear your voice:
silent is the dove in the cleft of the rock
and over is the time of singing.
The flowers are dead and gone;
only their essence lives on
in the oils with which I anoint your olive skin.
My fingers drip with liquid myrrh, my eyes with tears;
open was I to my love,
he waited at my door, eager to come in,
through the lattice he watched and called to me;
but my beloved has been taken;
and now my soul gasps and fails.

In the night they sought you,
they beat you and they wounded you,
my heart fainted within me;
now sleep escapes me
for my heart is broken open
like a forced door
and my inmost being yearns for you.
Gone are you from my touch
and no more may I hear the sound of your voice.
'Where has your beloved gone?'
my sisters ask.

My beloved has gone to his own locked garden,
his Spirit free, he waits for me
until the day breathes and the shadows flee
and then will I hold him and will not let him go,
but bring him into my mother's house,
into the chamber of her that conceived me.
Within will I bring him,
to dwell with me and within me,
a garden fountain, a well of living water,
for I am my beloved's and my beloved is mine.
Awake O North wind and come O South wind,
blow upon our garden and enliven it
as the holy breath of God unites all life in love.

* The imagery is taken from the Song of Songs

The apple tree*
My beloved is an apple tree
whose summer shade I have treasured gladly;
she is the kind, giving one
whose branches I have climbed,
generous and yielding
though I have surely taken
more than I deserve,
her fruit so good

* A medieval song describes Jesus Christ as an apple tree, an allusion to the Song of Songs.
Here I have connected this with the feminine aspect of Christ, since a fruit-bearing tree has
a distinctively feminine persona!

Rainbow God

My God is the richest purple of peace
and the most blissful blue,
sky blue, passion flower blue,
blue of jay's wing feathers
and flame's heart;
my God is forest green,
ocean green, green of peacock's
iridescent glory,
malachite green,
and the yellow of dandelions,
newest, tenderest leaves of beech,
peach flesh, orange of ripe,
luscious sweetness,
tiger lily flowers.
My God is red, red of moon blood,
red of ripe, wholesome goodness,
red of new life.
Beyond the red, beyond the purple
stretches colour I can
only dream;
Our God is spectrum,
and a prism the sacred scripture
of our rainbow hearts.

Prayer-walking the streets
A litany for the city

To love one another in a merciful, compassionate way is to engage with the mystery of God's love for us and in us and our own discovery of love for God. We who live in the ordinary world and are committed to the responsibilities of everyday life are called to a discipleship that is accessible to everyone, whether they have time on their hands or not. 'Love one another,' Jesus said, 'and then everyone will know you are my disciples.' Through our exploration of how to love and how not to love, we draw closer to God. There is a verse in the Song of Songs which brings together the mystical element of the lover's pursuit of the beloved and the call to go out into the city, into the busyness of everyday life and let that be the holy ground, our engagement with those we meet our active contemplation. I have used that verse to begin the litany that follows: *I will rise now and go about the city, in the streets and in the squares; I will seek him whom my soul loves …*

The litany arose out of a desire within our church community to surround the area with prayer following a street shooting. So a group began to meet to walk quietly around the area, stopping at significant places to pray, to sing and to light candles. As an extension to this, as Christmas time approached, some of us felt moved to take our prayer-walking into the city centre. The following litany is based on the one we used that evening. Since that time I have prayer-walked the city quite often, moved by the vulnerability of ordinary people going about their business, trusting in peace. Current world events show us the true fragility of the structures we have built up and the systems in which we place so much confidence – our 'false gods'; it has also exacerbated the sense of mistrust of and hostility against some sectors of our society, at a time when trust and mutual understanding are so important. When I walk on my own, my prayer is the Jesus prayer: *Lord Jesus, have mercy on me, a sinner.*

* * *

*   *change of speaker if more than one present*
    italic type: all

*   I will rise now and go about the city,
    in the streets and in the squares;
    I will seek him whom my soul loves.
    (Song of Songs 3:2)

God our soul's magnet,
may we be drawn to you,
fall in love with you,
follow you with a lover's devotion
through the gates of materialism and superficiality,
the exploitation and corruption,
the senseless waste of resources and the false gods,
to the humanity and the divinity
at the heart of the city.
Amen

* God who knows our hearts,
teach us not to judge,
lest we be judged.

Instead let us take willingly the ignorance,
the failure of imagination,
the selfishness,
the desperation,
the pressure,
the insecurity,
the anxiety,
the violence,
the prejudice,
the greed that we know within ourselves
and offer it up on behalf of all,
acknowledging our own weakness
and seeking a better way
in spite of ourselves.
This we ask in all humility,
Amen

* In shame we pray for those who suffer because of our weakness:

* For the sweatshop workers who make the goods we take for granted

* For children denied their childhood because they must slave for their daily bread

* For the producers of the raw materials, who are paid a pittance for their labour, for the sake of keeping the prices low

* For the machine operators and production-line workers who are banned from forming unions by the companies we support

* For all the victims, in our own city and in the wider world, of the economic system and power structures to which we subscribe

* For the vulnerable ones who come to our cities seeking refuge, and find only hostility and rejection

* For the earth, which groans under overburdened transport networks which bring the goods to the shelves

* For the air and water which are poisoned by unnecessary industry and transport, driven by consumer demand

* For our children and grandchildren, who will inherit the earth.

* *In shame we pray for your forgiveness, and for their forgiveness of us.*
  Renew a right spirit within us, O God
  and lead us to a better way,
  your Wisdom path of true peace and justice.
  Amen

* Lord have mercy,
  Christ have mercy,
  Lord have mercy.

Reflection:
* Who is my neighbour? the lawyer asked. Whom should I love with all my heart? And Jesus told a story of a traveller's mercy towards a victim of violent robbery, a victim from a different country, one hated by the traveller's own people. Who are our neighbours then? To whom can we bring Christ's merciful, healing love? Who are the victims of violence? Who have been robbed of their dignity, their empowerment and their voice? Who are the 'foreigners' in our midst, mistrusted and misunderstood, hated and feared? Who are the ones cast at the side of the road as though they are worthless? It is these who call us to kneel and serve; here are our neighbours. This is where discipleship is born.

* Hear what the Lord says of the great city to the prophet Jonah:

'And should I not be concerned about Nineveh, that great city, in which there are more than a hundred and twenty thousand people who do not know their right hand from their left ...?'

May we who seek find God's compassion in this city.
Show us how to give that compassion to our neighbours.

* Hear the words of John the Visionary:
And in the spirit he carried me away to a great, high mountain and showed me the holy city ... I saw no temple in the city, for its temple is the Lord God the Almighty and the Lamb. And the city has no need of sun or moon to shine on it, for the glory of God is its light, and its lamp is the Lamb. The nations will walk by its light, and the kings of the earth will bring their glory into it. Its gates will never be shut by day – and there will be no night there. People will bring into it the glory and the honour of the nations. (Revelation 21:10,22–26)

May we who seek find vision of a new way in this city.
Show us how to give hope to our neighbours.

* *Hear the words of Jesus, who wept over the city:*

As he came near and saw the city, he wept over it, saying, 'If you, even you, had only recognised on this day the things that make for peace! But now they are hidden from your eyes. (Luke 19:41–42)

May we who seek find God's peace in this city.
Show us how to give peace to our neighbours.

(Pause)

* Let us be still, and recognise the life and the love within the city: the diversity of peoples, the cultural wealth, the creative energy, the humour and the potential for good.

(Pause)

* Let us be still as we watch the people, busy with their own lives; people simply trying to make their lives work. Give us compassion, O God; remind us that these are all our neighbours.

(Pause)

* Let us be still as we feel for the homeless, the asylum-seekers and refugees, the lost, the lonely, the hungry and troubled, searching our own hearts for the compassion they need.

(Pause)

* Let us be still as we seek to understand the causes of violence, the troubled hearts of those who express themselves with acts of destruction. Let us seek ways in which healing might begin.

(Pause)

* Let us be still as we humble ourselves, knowing Jesus's words, that the prostitutes and the tax collectors with whom he spent his time will come to the Kingdom of God ahead those who consider themselves righteous.

(Pause)

> *'Blessed are you who are poor,*
> *for yours is the kingdom of God.*
> *'Blessed are you who are hungry now,*
> *for you will be filled.*
> *'Blessed are you who weep now,*
> *for you will laugh.*

* *'Blessed are you when people hate you, and when they exclude you, revile you, and defame you on account of the Son of Man. Rejoice on that day and leap for joy, for surely your reward is great in heaven; for that is what their ancestors did to the prophets.*

> *'But woe to you who are rich,*
> *for you have received your consolation.*
> *'Woe to you who are full now,*
> *for you will be hungry.*
> *'Woe to you who are laughing now,*
> *for you will mourn and weep.*
> *'Woe to you when all speak well of you,*
> *for that is what their ancestors did to the false prophets.*
> (Luke 6:20–26)

(Pause)

* We will rise now and go about the city,
in the streets and in the squares.

O God,
push us out of the comfortable
and onto the stony road;
show us a divided path and give us the choice
of which way to go.
Give us the freedom to be right and wrong,
then follow us, whichever way we go.
Amen

Chapter 8

THE WILD GOOSE

~ Come to me

About this chapter

This chapter reflects on the fact that although we may well spend much of our time operating as individuals, following our own agenda and concentrating on our own needs, we live interdependently. As with all people throughout time and around the world, we belong, however tightly or loosely, within community, a community which can be intimate yet radiates out in ever-increasing circles to encompass the whole planet, all life. Although we might well move on from one group, one place, one person, relationship doesn't end; rather it changes, and we change too. But in all our journeying God goes with us and the deepest communion of all never ends, only deepens. The big story behind this, as I see it, is one of the first and most familiar that we find in the book of Genesis, starting at chapter 12 – the story of Abram, called by God to leave his home town, to become the wandering, trusting ancestor through whom all people will be blessed.

The community of all life includes the lives that went before us and those to come. We belong together, brothers and sisters in relationship. A spiritual life is incomplete without an awareness of this interconnection, a sense of the impact we have on one another for good or ill, the realisation that we cannot love our neighbour completely until we love all. There are times when we find ways of recognising that togetherness, at least in part, by sharing food, song, story, silence, reflection and prayer, or by meeting another's need, but also further than that by connecting with and entering into communion with the creatures and plants of this earth, and with the earth itself. All life is our neighbour.

The ritualised Christian way of celebrating communion and expressing that journey together is to join in liturgical worship and I have included a eucharistic liturgy at the end of this book. Before that, though, I would like to explore alternative dimensions of spiritual communion, and how this can be celebrated or at least acknowledged in other ways.

A story

The following story is from the Chumash people of North America and I am telling it to illustrate the idea of being in and out of community, in and out of communion. Once you have read it, go back over it and notice the relationships the boy experiences: with his village, his family, the children, the geese, the racoon.

This is a story from the time when animals were closer to humans than they are now. In that time, there was a little boy who lived with his mother. When she remarried he found himself neglected and pushed out by the arrival of new little ones, and he was often hungry and ignored. So the boy decided nobody would miss him if he left, and he wandered away from home. He was still too young to be much good at looking after himself and was glad when he met up with another boy in a similar situation; they looked for food together, and Racoon came along to help them dig for roots, because Racoon was a kindly soul. More children came to join the group, and soon Racoon was taking care of seven. They camped out in the sweat lodge outside the village and every day they went down to the lake to drink and wash and catch fish; those fish, and the roots Racoon dug up from the earth, kept the children alive. At the lakeshore, they would meet every day with the wild geese, who were preparing to fly north to another land, where there was ripe grain to eat. They preened themselves carefully in preparation for the long journey, and cast their loose feathers on the ground. Well, the children liked the sound of this other land and wanted to go too. When the geese flew off, they gathered up the feathers cast onto the lakeshore, and stuck them all over their arms and backs. Round and round the outside of the sweat lodge they ran and danced, singing and laughing, children playing at flying, or children knowing that soon they would fly … After three days they began to rise into the air. Higher and higher they went, until they could look down on the whole village. They called to Racoon to come too, but he could not fly and had no wish to: he had already found his place of belonging and was content to stay. So they circled the village one last time, and the people down below noticed them and called out to them to come down. But the children had no wish to go back to that life, and went higher and higher. As they flew, they turned into geese; on and on they went, until they reached the heavens, where they found a place to be. They are there still, sitting together, and we can see them shining in the night sky – the constellation which people in the West call the Pleiades.

Comment

Like the story of Abram that we find in Genesis, this child's life is an interplay of entering into and moving out of communion with others, starting with the leaving of his unhappy home. First I want to look at the location for part of the story, the lakeside.

The shore in myth is often a mystical place, one of communion and journeying. The expanse of water that stretches out can be many things: the unknown future, the afterlife, the abode of spirits, the soul or dreaming mind, a meeting of heaven and earth, a point where mortals can go no further unless making their journey to the other world. In the Dream of Angus, the story for chapter 7, Angus reaches the shore of a lake and here meets his beloved, and is transformed so that both can fly together. In this chapter's story of the goose children, again we have transformation and flight, a journeying together into a spiritual dimension, and it is this spiritual connection which lasts.

In Christian scripture there are lots of real lakeshore moments, because Jesus spent such a lot of time around the lake of Galilee. We can even visit the shore of the stories, walk over the pebbles and sand, watch the boats, see the hills on the other side, and take a boat out ourselves and feel the wind and the waves. It is here that Jesus's fishermen disciples received the call to follow. Here too crowds gathered, hungry to hear Jesus's wisdom, and they stood on the shore at Capernaum as he spoke to them from a boat on the lake. In the Gospel of Matthew this story about preaching from a boat begins as Jesus left the house where he was staying to go and sit beside the sea for some time out. In Mark's version we are told that this follows a rather controversial healing. So Jesus went to the shore for peace and quiet, and there the crowds came, not to enter into his shalom but to hassle him for attention. It is here also, in John's gospel, that the disciples experience the risen Christ who stands on the beach calling them to share breakfast.

The shore then, in Christian terms, is the place where we come to hear the wisdom of Christ, to receive the call to discipleship, to be with Jesus in his own prayerfulness, and to partake of the meal which he prepares and calls those who love him to share. Affirming discipleship, entering into shalom together, receiving Jesus's wisdom, prayer in the Spirit and shared breaking of bread are what we do in our liturgy. Liturgy is a formalised script for our enactment of the shore experience, the point where we approach the great mystery of love together and are transformed by it so that we know freedom. The shore, literal or otherwise, is the arena of our communion. Many of these elements are somehow reflected in the Chumash story. But there are also many more non-scripted moments of lakeside experience, and these make up the spirituality of everyday life. They are the moments when we are touched deep down by a sense of gratitude, or compassion, or sorrow, or love, or empathy, for another living thing. It is easy to lose the moment, but it is also not that difficult to recognise it and celebrate the sacredness of communion with all we meet.

Soul friend

One day Jesus tries to bring his disciples away from the crowds for a while, and they set out by boat across the sea of Galilee, to a remote place. But people notice them going and walk around the shore, eager to meet Jesus. He has compassion on them, and there by the lake he teaches them. But the day draws on, the people are hungry, and the disciples have no food with them. As they are discussing what to do, a child comes forward, encouraged by Andrew, and gives Jesus his own food to share. Jesus takes what he offers and gives thanks, and as the food is distributed, somehow there is enough for everybody. In a chapter opening with a story about a little boy and his friends, that child of the gospel is soul friend for this chapter. As children we come to the shore, we offer all that we have and we share together with all in a great circle-dance of give and take.

Acts of communion

In previous chapters I have looked at body prayers, bead prayers, a covenant of salt and shrine-making, but in this chapter I would like to go a bit further into the idea of recognising holy moments of communion. What follows is a series of reflections on communion in the wider sense, suggested by encounters in the story of Abram and also that of the goose children. With each reflection is a suggestion for marking that communion with symbolic action or mini-liturgy, a way of acknowledging depth and sacredness of experience in everyday encounter. There is an account of Sioux medicine man Black Elk's visions, and how he communicated them to the people through drama and song. Only when he had given the visions to the people in this way, involving the people in their enactment, could their real value be drawn out. But he emphasised, in his description of the rituals, that it was the understanding of the action that gave the power, not the ritual itself. There was a deep truth expressed in story that could only be made real through its living-out by the people, but the actions were only the surface, leading to something deeper. Such is the nature of symbol: it points deeper, and you can use it at many levels. Creation of ritual, then, can be entirely superficial, or it can be entirely 'deep', depending on how you look at it. There is the surface of the lake, and there are the deep waters underneath.

The following are small actions which embody the truth of vision and story, altars to communion. In repetition they, and the words which accompany them, become something that lives in your heart, your subconscious. It is the treading many times of a path, until the route is clear: once you have made the path you will know the way back to that sure knowledge in your heart.

The primary communion, with God

To make God the priority looks like the undoing of communion. Abram walks away from his family home, Ur, a centre of a moon-worshipping cult. The child in the Chumash story leaves his family too. The call that inspires Abram is the call with which Jesus inspires his disciples: leave everything and follow me. It is the call into the unknown, the invitation into insecurity. That sounds frightening, threatening to all but those who, like the little boy, are suffering too much in their present state. But there are many levels to letting go – many little things we can release, many relationships based on grasping, clutching, insecure hanging-on, into which we can dare to invite God's Spirit of freedom. There are material things we can learn to relinquish, opinions and negative attitudes we can release, because they come between us and the God who calls for our attention. There are idols in which we falsely put our trust, fig-leaves of shame and fear and other barriers that can be shed in order to walk again with God. To do so, we have to decide to trust God above all community ties, above all family members, above all conventions and material securities. As a result, existing relationships will change, new relationships will grow, and we will develop new ways of looking at everything. It's interesting that two generations on from Abram, Rebecca left her father's household to start a new life with her husband Jacob, but she secretly brought the family idols with her. Perhaps they represented security to her, or protection, or blessing, or wealth, or fertility – something other than the complete surrender of walking into life with God. Surely we do the same: a totally clean break is more than we can contemplate and we hold on to something of our past because it still has value and meaning. We are not always ready to let go of everything; like Rebecca, we are often very human and imperfect in our surrender to God.

The first act, then, is to mark communion with God, to demonstrate trust through letting go – in other words, faith. I see it as like learning to swim by suddenly discovering that the water will support our weight if we let go. Suddenly the fear of drowning disappears in a moment of delightful weightlessness and all struggling ceases. There at the shore of the lake we look out at a great expanse of rippling, light-reflecting liquid and we are called to surrender everything. Using water is a very simple, lovely way to represent surrender to God. Take these words: Isaiah 46:4 *I have made, and I will bear; I will carry and will save.* Take water and something that floats, and bring them together somehow … that's it.

You might really stand at the seashore, and watch the waves, gaze out to the horizon, imagine yourself out in a boat on the sea; maybe even *be* in a boat … You might go to the swimming baths and just float with these words in your mind, or you might …

- Sit together in a group meditation where each person puts a cork in a bowl of water and somebody else says the words for them.
- Scoop up water from a stream and drop a petal into what you hold. The petal is yourself.
- Write the words on paper and float the paper.
- Go to a river and drop leaves or sticks into it as you say the words.
- Do any of the above and turn the words into a prayer or statement of faith: *You have made me, and you bear me, you carry and you save …*

Communion with place *(see chapter 2)*

Wherever Abram stopped on his journey, he built an altar to acknowledge God's presence at that place. One of the places where he built an altar was Bethel, 'house of God'. Wherever we are, God is. Wherever we go, God comes with us, is ahead of us, walks behind us. When we arrive at a place, we can remind ourselves that everywhere is Bethel, and as we travel we can remind ourselves that we too are Bethel on the move – we are temples of God's Holy Spirit. Altars are about offerings, sacrifices, releasing, relinquishing, letting go of something in acknowledgement that it actually belongs to God anyway. Altars are about thanksgiving, admission of remorse and plea for help. They are about recognising the sacredness of space, and they support our communion with God. The physical places where we stop are sites for altars, but so are the stages in our life journeys, the places we reach in our lives. All is sacred.

The way the patriarchs and matriarchs made altars was to set up a stone, so think about using stones and some of the words God spoke to Jacob as he dreamed of angels, his head resting on a stone which in the morning was to become an altar at Bethel. Jacob heard the same kind of promise as Abram: '*All the families of the earth shall be blessed in you and your offspring. Know that I am with you and will keep you wherever you go …*' (Genesis 28:14b–15a) You might …

- Keep a stone in your pocket: you are Bethel. As you walk, hold the stone and prayer-walk: '*Be with me and keep me wherever I go …*' or '*I thank you that always you are with me …*'
- Pick up a stone as you go, and lay it down with an offering to mark a significant moment …
- With respect to the Chumash story of the children, explore the symbolism of the four directions in Native American traditions. Begin by knowing yourself as the centre of an invisible circle, the circumference of which has no limit. North is the direction from which the cold winds and snow come; face it to pray

when you are suffering hardship. South is the road we take in death; face it when you are looking at death itself, physical separation and the vision–hope of life in the spirit, transcending the physical. West is the direction of the setting sun and the closure of things; it is a call to rest, a call to mature, a call to learn from the lessons of life, and to contemplate mortality. East is the direction of the rising sun, of Divine presence, of newness and gladness; face East when you are starting out on new ventures, when you want to be refreshed, when the risen Christ's presence calls you. Maybe place a witness stone marking the direction of your prayer. As you sit, stand or kneel in prayer, move through the four directions, your prayer changing with the mood of each, but always with the words of the promise at your centre: '*Know that I am with you and will keep you wherever you go ...*' (You might like to adapt the Daniel prayer at the end of chapter 6.)

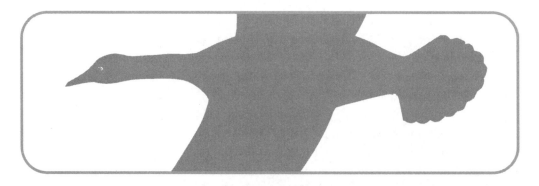

Communion of companionship

We can be Abram the visionary, travelling because we have heard God's call; or we can be Lot who goes because he trusts his wise companion and maybe sees an opportunity; or we can be Sara and go because of some kind of duty, obligation or bond of love; or we can be part of the entourage who go because they are dependants and don't have much choice ... (perhaps Sara belongs here actually). We have so many different relationships and the ones we have are always changing. How do we mark our respect for those with whom we travel? We can go to the first two people who used to walk together in the cool of the evening, in the presence of God, until one evening when God called, they hid instead of meeting up. When Adam walks with Eve it is in the knowledge of God; when Eve walks with Adam it is known to God. So it is: with whomever we journey, it is with God.

• Lay out parallel threads, string or sticks, each one representing a travelling companion of the present or the past, plus one for yourself. Let there be a space between each one, around which the Spirit of God can move freely, but let them be close and aligned. This is a picture of yourself where you are with those in your life. If you want to represent brokenness and discord, then do so with literal breaks and irregularities. Around the arrangement mark a circle, maybe scratched into the ground, or with a sprinkle of sand or a long cord … Let this represent the sacredness of the moment in which you are together. Place a lighted candle at the perimeter of the circle, or at the centre: you are held in God's love, surrounded by God's love, encompassed by God's love; God's love is the place where you came from and the place where you are going. There is nowhere else to go; God's Spirit upholds all, broken or whole.

Communion of self-honesty

Abram goes to Egypt because there is a famine in Canaan, and he lies that his wife is his sister because he is afraid that they will kill him and take her. Pharaoh does not want the guilt and the wrath of God that might be incurred accidentally, and he pays Abram to go away.

Abram is not morally superior; he is a normal human, putting his own interests first, amassing wealth, using others. Our communion with ourselves is self-honesty. We are no better than we should be, and when faced with challenge who knows what decisions we will make to protect ourselves? We are only human. Our actions have consequences for others and we are responsible for that. God does not judge or condemn Abram – it is Pharaoh who is angry with him and pays him to go away.

What do we do to mark honest communion with ourselves and acknowledgement of our self-interested or fear-based dealings with others?

- Notice things in which you can see your own reflection, both distorted and clear – a spoon, a shop window, a teapot, a puddle, a mirror, somebody's eyes, a glass, the communion wine … When you look at yourself, what do you think? Do you pass judgement? Do you smile, or frown? Reflect on 1 Corinthians 13:12–13 *For now we see in a mirror, dimly, but then we will see face to face. Now I know only in part; then I will know fully, even as I have been fully known. And now faith, hope, and love abide, these three; and the greatest of these is love.* Put it with the story in 1 Samuel 16:7 where Samuel is guided by God concerning which young man to anoint king: *But the Lord said to Samuel, 'Do not look on his appearance or on the height of his stature, because I have rejected him; for the Lord does not see as mortals see; they look on the outward appearance, but the Lord looks on the heart.'* Then Lamentation 2:19:

> *Arise, cry out in the night,*
> *at the beginning of the watches!*
> *Pour out your heart like water*
> *before the presence of the Lord!*

- Take all these thoughts and bring them together in action. Fill a container with a dark inner with water so that you can see your reflection. Gaze at yourself and let Paul's words become a prayer: *I thank you that I am fully known; I humble myself because I am fully known; Lord have mercy.*

   Pour out the water and use the words from Lamentations: *I pour out my heart to you, like water. Christ have mercy; Lord have mercy.*

   A time of quiet reflection or soul-searching might follow, closing with Paul's words: *I thank you that I am fully known; I humble myself because I am fully known; Lord have mercy.*

Communion of parting ways

Abram and Lot split because the land couldn't support both groups. The child in the Chumash story leaves his home because it is so full of unhappiness, and then later he and his friends leave Racoon and the village, to journey together. The geese leave because it is their instinct to travel according to the season and food supply.

Sometimes we journey together physically, sometimes it is necessary to go our separate ways. We can part painfully and it feels like losing a limb, or we can do it gracefully as part of the flow of living and dying and living again. Abram gives Lot choice of land and releases him on good terms with blessing and freedom.

How do we understand and act out our departures, our partings, our blessing of others, our letting go?

- Take a cord with several strands in it and place it inside a circle. The circle represents the ever-present love of God. The cord represents yourself and the person you feel bound to, tied to, attached to … whom you know you must let go.

   Then take the cord and separate out two strands – two identities, not one, two different directions – and lay them in different places in the circle. Doing so tells the story of the parting you know needs to take place and affirms that God is still with both people. God remains the beginning and end of all journeying. It may be that you stay close, that you will be reunited in the future, or that the physical distance will continue, but always the imprint of the other will remain present in the twisting of the string, and always the Holy Spirit will move around and between both in blessing. So, as Abram says, 'Let there be no strife between us.'

Communion of power

In the story of Abram and Lot, shortly after their parting Lot is taken captive and Abram dashes off to rescue him. It's a story about power and how someone with plenty helps someone who has none. Many of our encounters with others reflect this dynamic: we seem either to be the powerful one or the powerless one, and we can use both situations to help or to abuse. But beneath superficial appearances, always there is God the Great Leveller, from whom all true power proceeds. Whatever we do to try to rescue another, or establish justice as we see it, it needs to be through the energy of the Holy Spirit. There is no space for self-glorification. And likewise, if we feel ourselves rescued, thanks is due to the person acting in the power of the Spirit, but thanks is also due to the Spirit herself.

- Meditate on a pair of scales which are out of balance because the weight does not match the load. Find a set, and physically play with them; imprint the sense of balance and imbalance in your mind. Your role is either to reduce the weights or to increase them so that balance is achieved. This is a meditation that can be used to reflect any activity that has an impact on others, whether as Lot or as Abram, powerful or powerless, and it gives a sense of the underlying equality of all and the all-powerfulness of God. It also 'draws the picture' of restoring equality. In the words of the Magnificat, if you give of your might to raise up the lowly you work towards equality.

- There are rituals in a number of cultures which use earth on the body: for example, in Islam, if water is not available to wash before prayers then earth can be used; in Sioux culture, earth might be applied to the forehead before action, to remind the person that it is not their power but the Great Spirit's that they use. When you know you have to do something 'powerful' that will have an impact on another, take some earth and hold it in your hand, then moisten a finger and use it to pick up enough of the earth to make a mark on your forehead or the back of your hand: *We are all of the earth and to the earth we return; it is the Spirit which breathes in us that has the power to heal and to help. Amen*

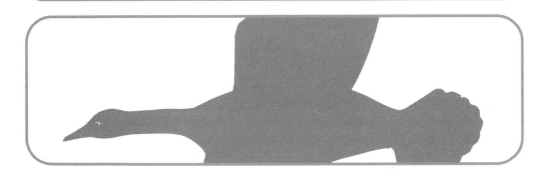

Communion of equals

A story much beloved of the early church, as we see by reading the book of Hebrews, is the meeting between Abram and Melchizedek, priest-king of Salem. Salem is thought to mean Peace (sharing the same root SLM as the Hebrew Shalom, Arabic Salaam, Aramaic Shalama), and the city is now known as Jerusalem. In the story Melchizedek is Priest of God Most High, El Elyon, a name we find elsewhere referring to the God of the Bible. El was the ancient Canaanite word for God; it was also the name of the father of the gods in the Canaanite religion, and it is found throughout the Hebrew scriptures wherever translators give the word *God*. (Where they use Lord, it is the name Yahweh they are indicating.) El is related to the Arabic Allah, and the Aramaic Allaha, which Jesus would have used. Melchizedek, then, is a holy figure who draws together the three faith traditions of Abraham – Judaism, Islam and Christianity – and he does so in the city of Peace, using the ritual of a shared meal. While the name of the nation is Israel, which means *he who strives with God,* the city at its heart is Peace, and it is a meeting place for blessing and respect for those following different paths but sharing their devotion to God Most High, by whatever name.

The communion inspired by the meeting of Abram and Melchizedek is the communion of respect and the desire for peace between peoples. It is at once celebrating difference and points of meeting.

A specifically Christian enactment of the story is the communion, the sharing of bread and wine. But the Melchizedek story asks us to keep open table, to welcome rather than exclude, to meet and share, to explore mutual respect, and this offers comment on the manner in which we celebrate our Eucharist.

- Read the vision of the New Jerusalem in Revelation 21:9–22:7: it is a place where the nations will walk by the light of God's glory and of the lamb, a place where there is no temple but only this light, a place from which flows the river of life, with trees of healing along its banks. Explore the ideas in the vision; try drawing or painting them, or arranging objects into a mandala form: a circle divided into twelve for the twelve gates, a lamb at the heart, the presence of people of all nations, a river flowing out … It doesn't matter whether your picture looks 'good' or not – there is no 'right' way of doing it. Drawing is a process of expressing your thinking. It is for you alone, an active meditation which you can return to often, to change as new thoughts come to you.

Communion of stars

God's blessing on Abraham, that his descendants will be countless, is illustrated in a beautiful way: God brought him outside and said, *'Look towards heaven and count the stars if you are able ...'* God speaks through the natural. God asks us to look with awe at the natural world, and to listen to what it tells us, to let it teach us about God. This in itself – the simplest contemplation, the timeless call to 'commune with nature' – is a meeting point, a learning, a deepening of faith.

Abram looks and he believes God's promise. It makes sense to him, seeing the vastness of the universe. We too are simply called to come outside and look, maybe at the stars, maybe the sea – or the trees, or the desert – and wait for what they tell us of God; wait for the prayer of humility and awe to well up from within, prayer as in the spirit of Job, faced with the power of God. *'I have uttered what I did not understand, things too wonderful for me, which I did not know.'* (Job 42:3b). We are to notice the vast and the tiny, from the night sky to a grain of salt, from thunderstorms to wind humming in telegraph wires – the microscopic and the macroscopic – and to remember that God's blessing is for all creation. So keep a magnifying lens in your pocket, the knowledge in mind that all life is our neighbour, this earth the home we share, and the name of God in your heart: I AM.

Communion of discipleship: preparation

This chapter draws to a close with a form of communion that has been used for various gatherings: an evening worship group, a retreat, a conference exploring Christianity and Anarchism ... situations where people draw together to explore the sanctity of togetherness in new ways. The idea of this liturgy is that a group gathering in the name of Jesus is free to share peace, to give thanks and to break bread together, in the promise that when two or more gather in the name of Jesus, he is there with them. This is ancient belief and practice among Christians and, as in the oldest gatherings, the only requirement for joining in is wanting to. Anyone who wishes to draw closer to Jesus in this way, to pray and to share bread with others is welcome, whatever their age, denomination, sexual preference, financial situation, status and so on. In Christ there is neither slave nor free, male nor female, young nor old, rich nor poor, gay nor straight ... (An updated rendering of Galatians 3:28–29). There is, then, a desire in all present to explore equality before Christ.

Although the earliest church had the apostles, prophets and administrative deacons, there were no priests as such. Jesus himself cautioned against calling others Rabbi, the title for official spiritual leaders of the time: all were disciples, equal in Christ. I am not proposing that we go back to this situation as such, for priesthood has now become a sacred role. But here I offer a radical (in the true sense of the word) way in which a group of 'ordinary' people can share thanksgiving with confidence, drawing from the roots and scriptures of our faith, using a structure which follows a traditional act of worship. There is no one special prayer that only one person can say, no particular sacred ritual that can only be enacted by an ordained individual. All words, all actions, are shared out among the group.

Preparation for worship

This worship can be shared in a house-group setting, on a beach, in a field, in a car park or anywhere else where there is space and people find it easy to gather – perhaps even in a church! It will work best with at least six people, so that all the roles are taken by different individuals and the dancing works well, but if only two are participating they can alternate parts. For a group larger than twenty or so, the liturgy will need practical adaptations, for example during the hand-washing.

I have included three short readings in the text on the theme of the chapter. It is best to choose short passages of scripture to suit the occasion for which the liturgy is being used. The 'different' version of the Lord's Prayer is my own re-translation from the Greek of the prayer as it is found in Luke's Gospel, using alternative ancient manuscripts. I have also included songs which I wrote myself, although on two occasions, when people had gathered from far and wide, it seemed more appropriate to substitute Taizé songs that most would know.

Preparation
- Lots of stones, at least enough for one each
- Seven candles in a bowl of sand or holder, one larger candle to be lit from the beginning, and extra candles for individuals to light
- For the hand-washing: a bowl of water and a hand towel (or several, depending on numbers)
- For the meal, non-alcoholic wine (or something similar) in a cup, bread roll or equivalent on a plate
- Appropriate background music to set the tone at the beginning

This is probably the only part which might require a bit of clear leadership!
It is necessary to devote time, perhaps fifteen minutes or so before the worship itself, to learn the songs and the dance. If children are involved, they might like to learn it in advance, so they are able to teach it to everyone else.

The Shalom dance is easy! *Start by joining hands in a circle.*
Shalom, shalom, shalom, *three steps to the right (note main beat is on the 'lom!)*
My peace I give to you. *three steps to the left*
Shalom, shalom, shalom, shalom, *two steps inward, on the first and third shalom*
My peace I give to you. *two steps back, on* peace *and* you

Other songs to learn: 1.*For you to be with us,* 2. *As we forgive,* 3. *The broken body of Jesus,* 4. *Shalom, shalom (dance)*
These are best sung unaccompanied.

The liturgy is read in rotation around the circle by all members of the group. Members of the clergy present can of course contribute too, since they share equality with everyone else, but it is in the spirit of the service for them to decline invitations to take a lead, as there is no lead to be taken!

italic type is for everyone to say
asterisk * denotes change of reader, rotating right around the group.
hash # denotes change of active participation roles, rotating around the group.
Before the worship begins, place a card with a * and a card with a # on different seats in the circle. Whoever sits in these places will be first reader and first active participant.

Leaderless Eucharist

Opening

* In the name of Jesus we are gathered.
   Then Jesus is here with us.

* May his spirit stir our hearts with love.
   Jesus, we welcome you;
   Spirit, we welcome you;
   God of all, we welcome you.

   Sing together:
   For you to be with us
   is our hearts' deepest desire;
   here with us you are –
   does not our spirit stir within?   x3

For you to be with us is our hearts' deep-est de - sire;____

here with us you are — does not our spi - rit stir with - in?

Canticle from Psalm 146

*   Praise the Lord!
    Praise the Lord, O my soul!

*   I will praise the Lord as long as I live;
    I will sing praises to my God all my life long.

*   Do not put your trust in princes,
        in mortals, in whom there is no help.
    When their breath departs, they return to the earth;
        on that very day their plans perish.

*   Happy are those whose help is the God of Abraham,
        whose hope is in the Lord their God,
    who made heaven and earth,
        the sea, and all that is in them;

*   who keeps faith for ever;
    who executes justice for the oppressed;
    who gives food to the hungry.

*   The Lord sets the prisoners free;
    the Lord opens the eyes of the blind.

*   The Lord lifts up those who are bowed down;
    the Lord loves the righteous.

*   The Lord watches over the strangers;
    he upholds the orphan and the widow.

*   The Lord will reign for ever,
    Praise the Lord!

Prayer of reconciliation

Each person takes a stone.

* How can we have room for God's love in our hearts, when our hearts are full already?
These stones from the sea shore,
they are our worries.
They are the hurts we have caused others.
They are the unkind words we have said.
They are our selfishness and greed.
They weigh down our hearts.
These stones are our worries.
They are the hurts we have felt
through the words and behaviour of others.
They are the burdens we have taken up
and suffered over.
They weigh down our hearts.

* Let us meditate on the things which weigh down our hearts.

Pause in silence

* *Holding up stone* Let us give up all these things that make our hearts heavy. Let us offer them to God, who makes all things new.

God of Peace, lighten our hearts; forgive us and heal us. Amen

Everyone places their stone close to the central candle, then stands in a circle.

God of Jesus,
your love is the love of a mother
who adores her children and forgives them everything.
Your love is the love of a father
who is devoted to his children and accepts them always.
We are your children.
We fall down and you help us up.
We go wrong and you put us right.
Now, fill our emptiness with your love,
replace our brokenness with wholeness,
our weakness with your strength,

that we may go out into the world and be of use to you.
Amen

* God is a God of forgiveness. So let us reassure one another by singing:
As we forgive others, so God forgives us;
I forgive and am forgiven.   x3

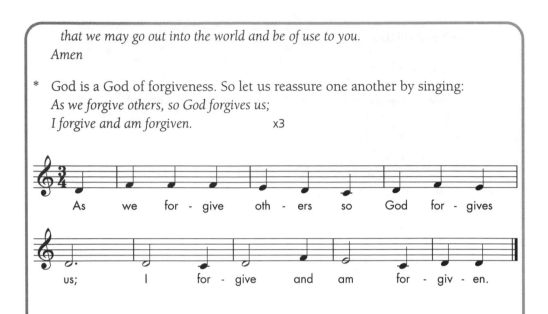

As   we   for - give   oth - ers   so   God   for - gives
us;   I   for - give   and   am   for - giv - en.

* Let us share together the peace which comes from God:

All share a sign of peace, then return to seats.

* Hear the word of God, who spoke through the Hebrew scriptures:

Now the Lord said to Abram, 'Go from your country and your kindred and your father's house to the land that I will show you. I will make of you a great nation, and I will bless you, and make your name great, so that you will be a blessing. I will bless those who bless you, and the one who curses you I will curse; and in you all the families of the earth shall be blessed.' (Genesis 12:1–3)

May God speak to our hearts.

* Hear the word of the Gospel:
Jesus departed with his disciples to the lake, and a great multitude from Galilee followed him; hearing all that he was doing, they came to him in great numbers from Judea, Jerusalem, Idumea, beyond the Jordan, and the region around Tyre and Sidon. He told his disciples to have a boat ready for him because of the crowd, so that they would not crush him; for he had cured many, so that all who had diseases pressed upon him to touch him. Whenever the unclean spirits saw him, they fell down before him and shouted, 'You are the Son of God!' But he sternly ordered them not to make him known. (Mark 3:7–12)

May Christ speak to our hearts.

* Hear the word of the apostles:

Let love be genuine; hate what is evil, hold fast to what is good; love one another with mutual affection; outdo one another in showing honour. Do not lag in zeal, be ardent in spirit, serve the Lord. Rejoice in hope, be patient in suffering, persevere in prayer. Contribute to the needs of the saints; extend hospitality to strangers.

Bless those who persecute you; bless and do not curse them. Rejoice with those who rejoice, weep with those who weep. Live in harmony with one another; do not be haughty, but associate with the lowly; do not claim to be wiser than you are. Do not repay anyone evil for evil, but take thought for what is noble in the sight of all. If it is possible, so far as it depends on you, live peaceably with all. (Romans 12:9–18)

May the Holy Spirit speak to our hearts.

Statement of faith and commitment

Mother–Father God, by your infinite love,
all is conceived and brought to birth,
all life animated by your breath,
all souls embraced by the outstretched arms
of your son, our brother.
We stand together,
to offer ourselves as caretakers of your creation,
keepers of the Word,
emissaries of Christ's peace.
And so we journey on,
lovers of life, lovers of Christ,
lovers of your Great Mystery,
living and dying and embracing new life,
ever closer to our home in you.
Amen

Intercession:

*   Let us pause now, to let our love of others grow and spread out to all the world.

With each statement a different person *starting with #*, then rotating around the circle, lights a candle before the prayer continues.

* Let us remember the ones who are hungry.
Teach us how to share, O God.

Pause for candle-lighting

* Let us remember the ones who have no home.
Let us welcome them.

Pause for candle-lighting

* Let us remember those who don't have proper clothes to wear.
Let us give from our own abundance.

Pause for candle-lighting

* Let us remember those who are lonely, or grieving.
Let us reach out in friendship.

Pause for candle-lighting

* Let us remember those who are afraid and those in pain.
May we give our tenderness and our compassion.

Pause for candle-lighting

* Let us remember those who have lost their freedom to others.
Let us bring to them the freedom and equality of all in Christ.

Pause for candle-lighting

* Let us pray for ourselves as we go about our daily lives.
Fill us with the gentleness and strength of your Spirit.
Amen

Pause for candle-lighting

* We each have our own prayers to offer to God; let our prayers be like lights in the darkness.

Individuals can come up to light their own candles, with or without spoken prayers.

After a pause the next speaker stands/sits/kneels back in the circle to indicate all should do the same.

* We open our hearts to God's love.
We open our hearts to God's love.

* Our love is for one another.
Our love is for one another.

* Our love is for the unlovely.
Our love is for the unlovely.

* Our love is for all the world.
Our love is for all the world.

Amen

Peace

This Shalom can be sung while dancing slowly in a circle, holding hands. Dance steps described in preparation section at start of liturgy.

All: *Shalom, shalom, shalom,*
       My peace I give to you.
       Shalom, shalom, shalom, shalom,
       My peace I give to you.   x4 or more!

* Let us remember how Jesus took a bowl and, kneeling, washed the feet of his followers.
Anyone who wishes to be great in the eyes of God must be the servant of all.

Hand-washing follows. Move to stations around the room where bowls of water are placed, and take turns to wash one another's hands. When all who want to have taken part:

*   We are children together of one God,
we are brothers and sisters together,
shoulder to shoulder with all peoples and with all life.
Not because we are special,
not because we are proud do we stand here,
but because God has welcomed each of us
just as we are.
We give thanks that we are acceptable to God,
included in God's love,
enlivened by the Holy Spirit,
welcomed by Jesus into fellowship,
invited to draw close
and to share in the gift of eternal life.
Amen

goes to the table, and lifts up the bread, breaking it at the appropriate moment, **then stays there.**

All: *We remember the Last Supper which Jesus shared with his followers, on the night before he died. 'And as they ate, he took a loaf of bread and gave thanks. He broke it, and gave the bread to them, saying, "Take, this is my body." '*

Sing meditatively together:
The broken body of Jesus,
the blood of the Prince of Peace;
how can we forget
the gift of his life?
May his life live on in our love.   x3

Next # also goes to the table and takes the cup in her or his hands, staying with the bread-breaker.

All: *Then he took a cup, and after giving thanks he gave it to them, and all of them drank from it. He said that the wine was his blood, sealing the bond of forgiveness between God and humanity.*

The two ## hold up the bread and wine until the song is over:

All: *Jesus told his followers to remember him by sharing bread and wine. So let us remember our teacher. Let us remember his words, his deeds, his death and his resurrection, with thanksgiving. Amen*

Sing together:
> *The broken body of Jesus,*
> *the blood of the Prince of Peace;*
> *how can we forget*
> *the gift of his life?*
> *May his life live on in our love.*   x3

All: (kneeling or heads bowed)
> *Spirit of God be around us*
> *and within us,*
> *close as the air we breathe.*
> *Whisper over these gifts,*
> *fruits of the earth*
> *changed by human hands,*
> *that to us they may be*
> *spiritual food and drink.*
>
> *God, the Father and Mother of us all,*
> *may your name be respected as holy.*
> *May your kingdom come,*
> *may your Holy Spirit overcome us and guide us.*
> *Give us each day our bread for tomorrow,*
> *and forgive us our sins*
> *as we release all who are indebted to us.*
> *Spare us from temptation*
> *and wrench us away from evil.*
> *Amen*

Distribution

Next two ## take the bread and wine back to their seats. The bread is passed first around the circle, with the words: *'Eat with thanks.'* After a pause, the wine follows in the same direction: *'Drink and remember.'*

The cup and plate are then placed back on the table. If there is bread or wine left, it can be shared out after worship.

Repeat opening canticle:
For you to be with us
is our hearts' deepest desire;
here with us you are –
does not our spirit stir within?   x3

All stand in circle.

*   Let us give thanks.

All: *God our Mother and our Father,*
          thank you for feeding us our daily bread,
          and for the spiritual food and drink which we receive
          through Jesus your servant, our brother.
          Thank you that he lived on earth to show the way,
          that he died true to his message of love
          and returned to life, to fill us with hope.
          Keep us strong in our daily lives,
          to show the love of Jesus
          in all we do, think and say.
          Amen

*   Let us bless one another as we prepare to go out into the world.

All turn to the people on either side in the circle. To give blessing, hold the other person's hands in your own and say *Be strong in God's love.* With the reply *Amen.*

POSTSCRIPT

Like Angus in the story of the swan maiden, we find ourselves on a journey towards what we truly want. The nature of what we want only becomes apparent to us gradually, and often, faced with the derision and incomprehension of others, it takes courage to commit to the path of love rather than the path of materialistic self-serving.

In asking myself *How does one live an ordinary life in a spiritual way?* I searched all over the place and I am still looking for an answer. I probably always shall be. But along the way three principles or rules seem to keep reappearing like great witness stones on a landscape – not new ones, ancient ones – and they in turn prompt not answers to my question, but more questions. They are not rules we can obey easily and tick off as achievements; they are more like ongoing challenges.

Three rules of life

The three main rules are summarised by Paul's advice: 'Make love your aim.' (1 Corinthians 14:1) The first two are at the heart of the Hebrew scriptures and were singled out by Jesus as the essence of all other laws. The laws came into existence to help people live out their love of God and one another, and obedience to the law was meant to be a joy: love in action. The third rule is an expression of this, from Paul whose life was transformed by finding an unexpected love.

- Love God with all your heart, soul, mind and strength. (Deuteronomy 6:5)
- Love your neighbour as you love yourself. (Leviticus 19:18)
- Let all that you do be done in love. (1 Corinthians 16:14)

These rules are approached in three principal ways: through prayer, through relationship and through activity. Daily life needs to include all three – but how? Can we structure the journey? Can we find ourselves a pattern, a rule of life that anchors us and keeps us secure; a map that guides us along the way? Can we challenge ourselves to take on discipline and so move on with greater confidence and energy? These are questions which lead only to more questions, but the ultimate answer surely lies at the heart of life.

Prayer

How often should we pray? What kind of prayers should we use? What doors can we open to hearing God's word? What kind of discipline is it right to impose on ourselves? What is the balance between Jesus's teaching to pray in private, and to commit ourselves to regular prayer? Can we connect our prayer life to the seasons of the church year, or the seasons of the earth's year, or both? How and when might we use body prayers such as the Daniel prayer, silent openness, prayer beads, mantras, or intercession, including prayer for those who seem to be in opposition to us? Since God looks at the heart, is it a prayer if we act with love? How do we deal with the times we feel distanced from God?

Relationship

How should we approach each relationship? As a brother, a sister, a mother, a lover? How do we recognise and honour the presence of God in others and ourselves? What does our dress, our diet, our behaviour communicate to others? What decisions can we make about our lifestyle to alter the effect it has on others? In empathising with others, can we aim to wear only fair-trade clothes and eat cruelty-free food? Can we minimise our use of resources? Can we live out Jesus's teaching to avoid judging others and not to be self-righteous? Can we learn true compassion, gratitude and appreciation? Can we recognise those who are marginalised, rejected, despised and misunderstood and go to them in loving service? How might we respond lovingly to those who challenge us, even attack us? How do we deal with our failings, our moments of lovelessness?

Action

In trying to love what we do, can we become reconciled with the things that are distasteful to us? Can we change what we do so that it becomes easier to love? Can we change our attitude, our expectations, our motivation, our routine? Can prayer enter into our activity? Can our activity be connected to our relationships? How might we find God in what we do? Can we rid ourselves of materialistic motivation, greed, power-seeking and self-interest? Can our action become motivated by the desire to serve? How might we serve without becoming servile? How can love permeate *everything* we do? How can we become more open to the presence of the Holy Spirit, Ruah, in what we do? How can we use our gifts and strengths? How can we work with our weaknesses?

The answers to these questions are different for each of us and they change every day, but always the three rules stand as constants in a world of confusion and change. Our journey to love is no wild goose chase but the one journey of true worth. Only by committing ourselves to the path do we realise that the love we seek is already within us, calling us on.

And why do you worry about clothing? Consider the lilies of the field, how they grow; they neither toil nor spin, yet I tell you, even Solomon in all his glory was not clothed like one of these. But if God so clothes the grass of the field, which is alive today and tomorrow is thrown into the oven, will he not much more clothe you – you of little faith? Therefore do not worry, saying, 'What will we eat?' or 'What will we drink?' or 'What will we wear?' For it is the Gentiles who strive for all these things; and indeed your heavenly Father knows that you need all these things. But strive first for the kingdom of God and his righteousness, and all these things will be given to you as well.

Matthew 6:28–35

Also from Wild Goose Publications ...

Reclaiming the Sealskin
Meditations in the Celtic Spirit
Annie Heppenstall-West

A book of meditations inspired by the Celtic legend of the selkie, a mythical seal-like creature who could also live on land in human form but sometimes became trapped because a human stole its sealskin. The selkie's vast nameless longing for the ocean is analogous to the soul's longing for the ocean of God.

Seventy contemplations on the natural world and some human-made objects make up the core of the book. Each reflects on body, mind and spirit in relation to the subject and finishes with a prayer.

In the spirit of modern Celtic Christianity, one of the purposes of this book is to discover parallels between traditional scripture and the contemplation of nature, and to harmonise the two. Sometimes – perhaps influenced by the fear and suspicion associated with the witch hunts of previous centuries – Christians are reluctant to bond too closely with the natural world. This author believes that the creatures and plants around us have a voice to help us in our search for the sealskin, our spiritual freedom.

Includes full-colour meditation cards that can be detached and used as an aid to meditation.

ISBN 1-901557-66-9

See all our publications at
www.ionabooks.com

The Iona Community is ...

- An ecumenical movement of men and women from different walks of life and different traditions in the Christian church
- Committed to the gospel of Jesus Christ, and to following where that leads, even into the unknown
- Engaged together, and with people of goodwill across the world, in acting, reflecting and praying for justice, peace and the integrity of creation
- Convinced that the inclusive community we seek must be embodied in the community we practise

Together with our staff, we are responsible for:

- Our islands residential centres of Iona Abbey, the MacLeod Centre on Iona, and Camas Adventure Centre on the Ross of Mull

and in Glasgow:

- The administration of the Community
- Our work with young people
- Our publishing house, Wild Goose Publications
- Our association in the revitalising of worship with the Wild Goose Resource Group

The Iona Community was founded in Glasgow in 1938 by George MacLeod, minister, visionary and prophetic witness for peace, in the context of the poverty and despair of the Depression. Its original task of rebuilding the monastic ruins of Iona Abbey became a sign of hopeful rebuilding of community in Scotland and beyond. Today, we are about 250 Members, mostly in Britain, and 1500 Associate Members, with 1400 Friends worldwide. Together and apart, 'we follow the light we have, and pray for more light'.

For information on the Iona Community contact:
The Iona Community, Fourth Floor, Savoy House, 140 Sauchiehall Street,
Glasgow G2 3DH, UK. Phone: 0141 332 6343
e-mail: admin@iona.org.uk; web: www.iona.org.uk

For enquiries about visiting Iona, please contact:
Iona Abbey, Isle of Iona, Argyll PA76 6SN, UK. Phone: 01681 700404
e-mail: ionacomm@iona.org.uk

Wild Goose Publications, the publishing house of the Iona Community established in the Celtic Christian tradition of Saint Columba, produces books, tapes and CDs on:

- holistic spirituality
- social justice
- political and peace issues
- healing
- innovative approaches to worship
- song in worship, including the work of the Wild Goose Resource Group
- material for meditation and reflection

If you would like to find out more about our books, tapes and CDs, please contact us at:

Wild Goose Publications
Fourth Floor, Savoy House
140 Sauchiehall Street,
Glasgow G2 3DH, UK

Tel. +44 (0)141 332 6292
Fax +44 (0)141 332 1090
e-mail: admin@ionabooks.com

or visit our website at
www.ionabooks.com
for details of all our products and online sales